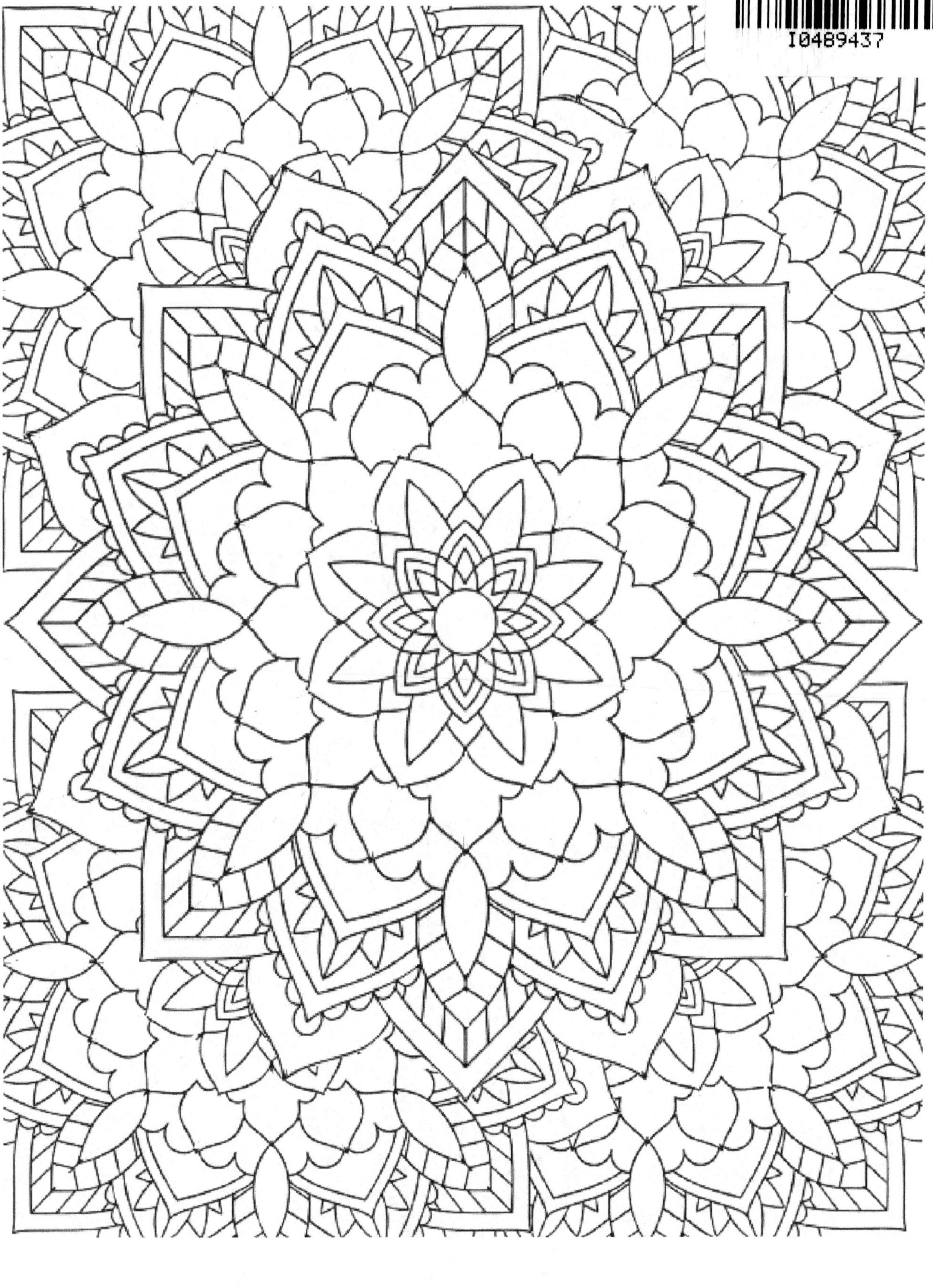

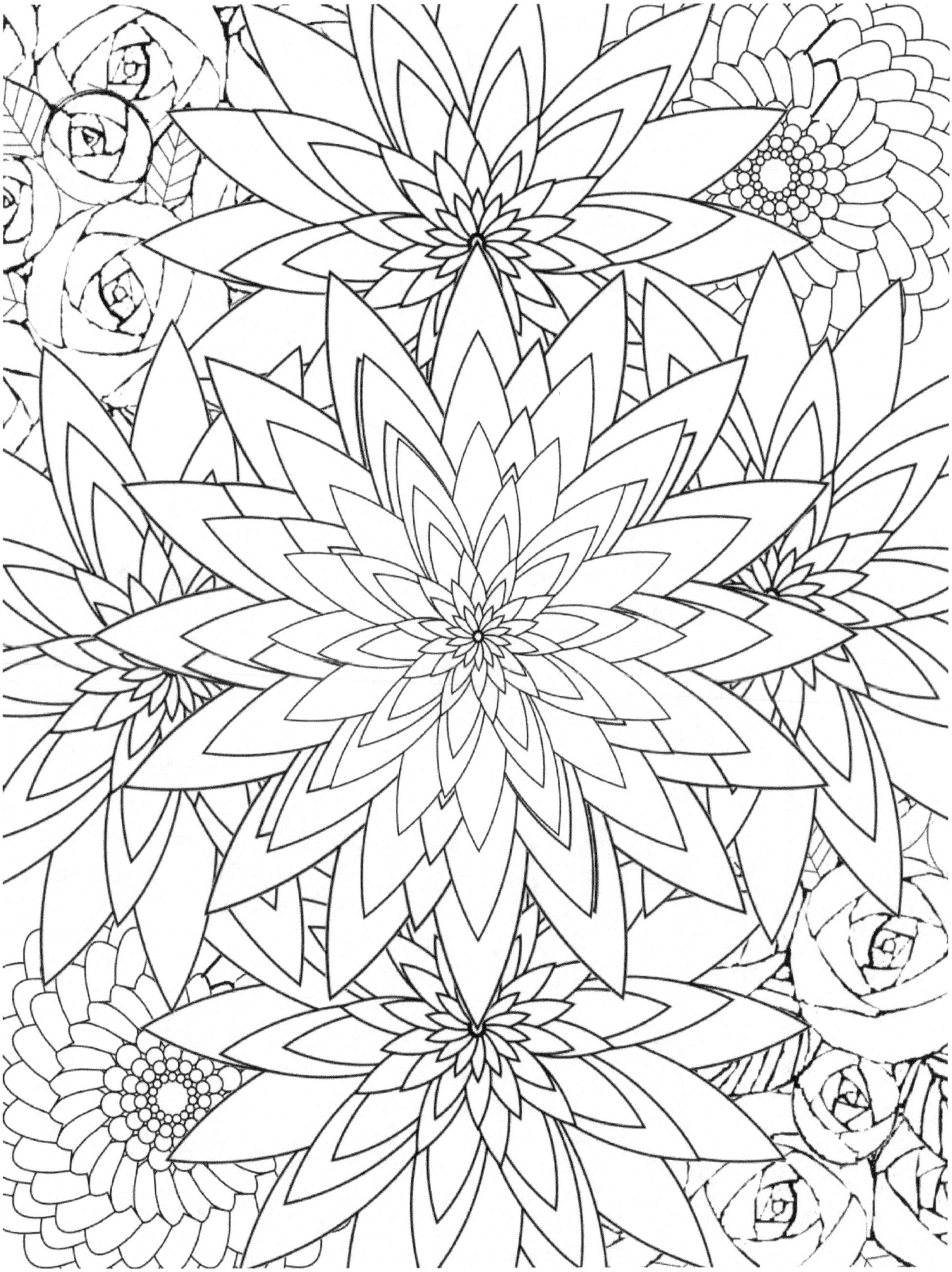

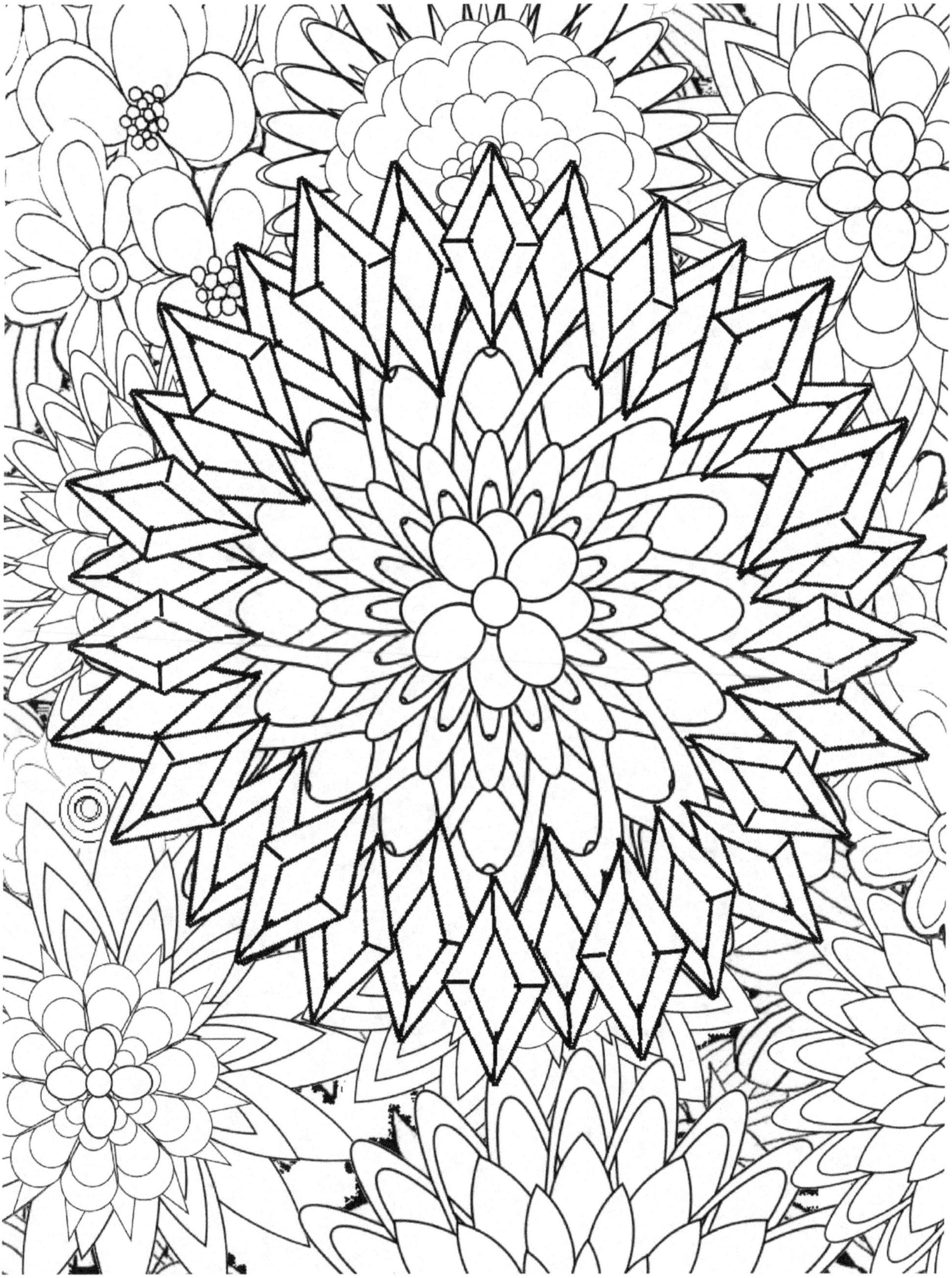

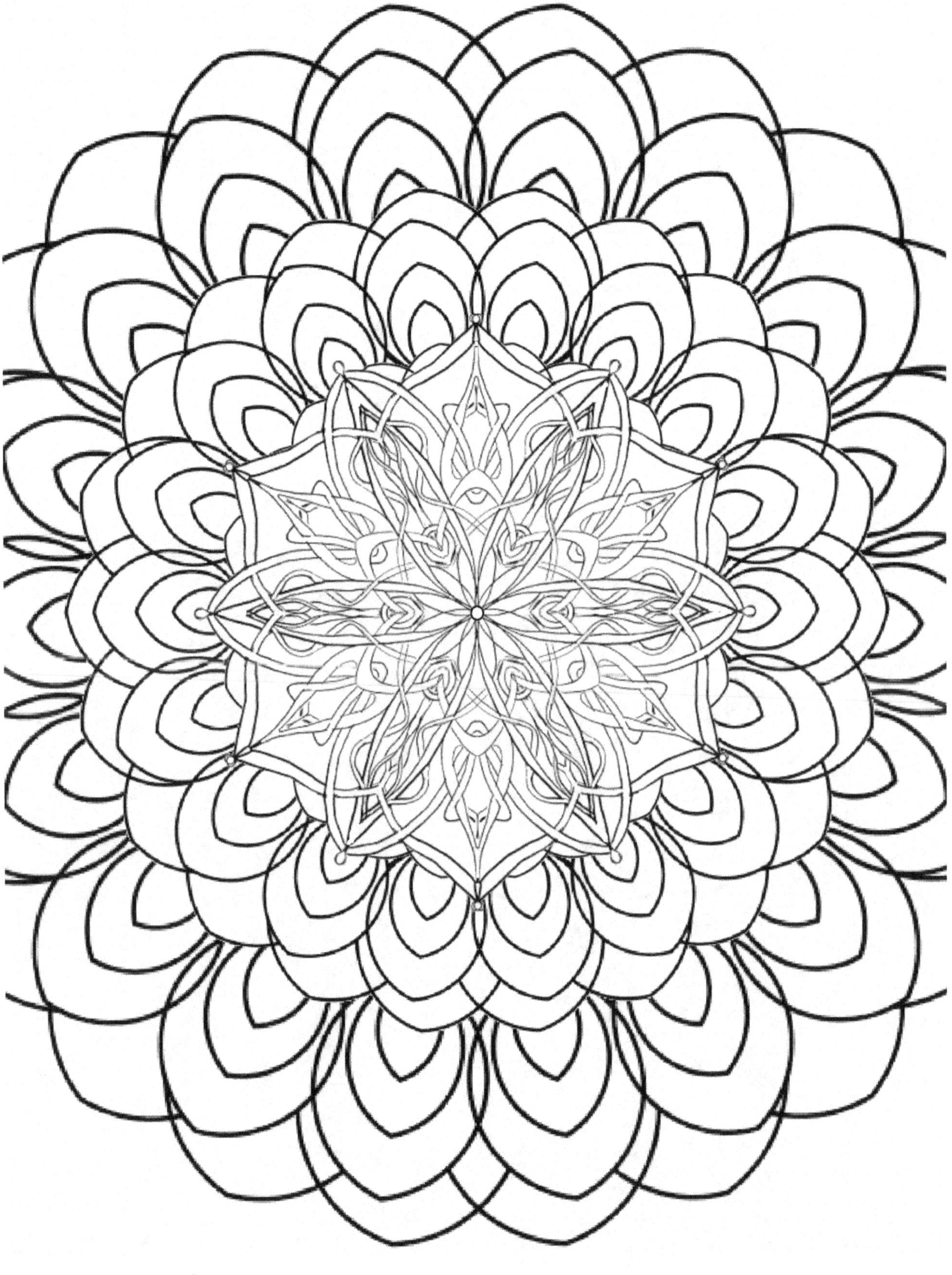

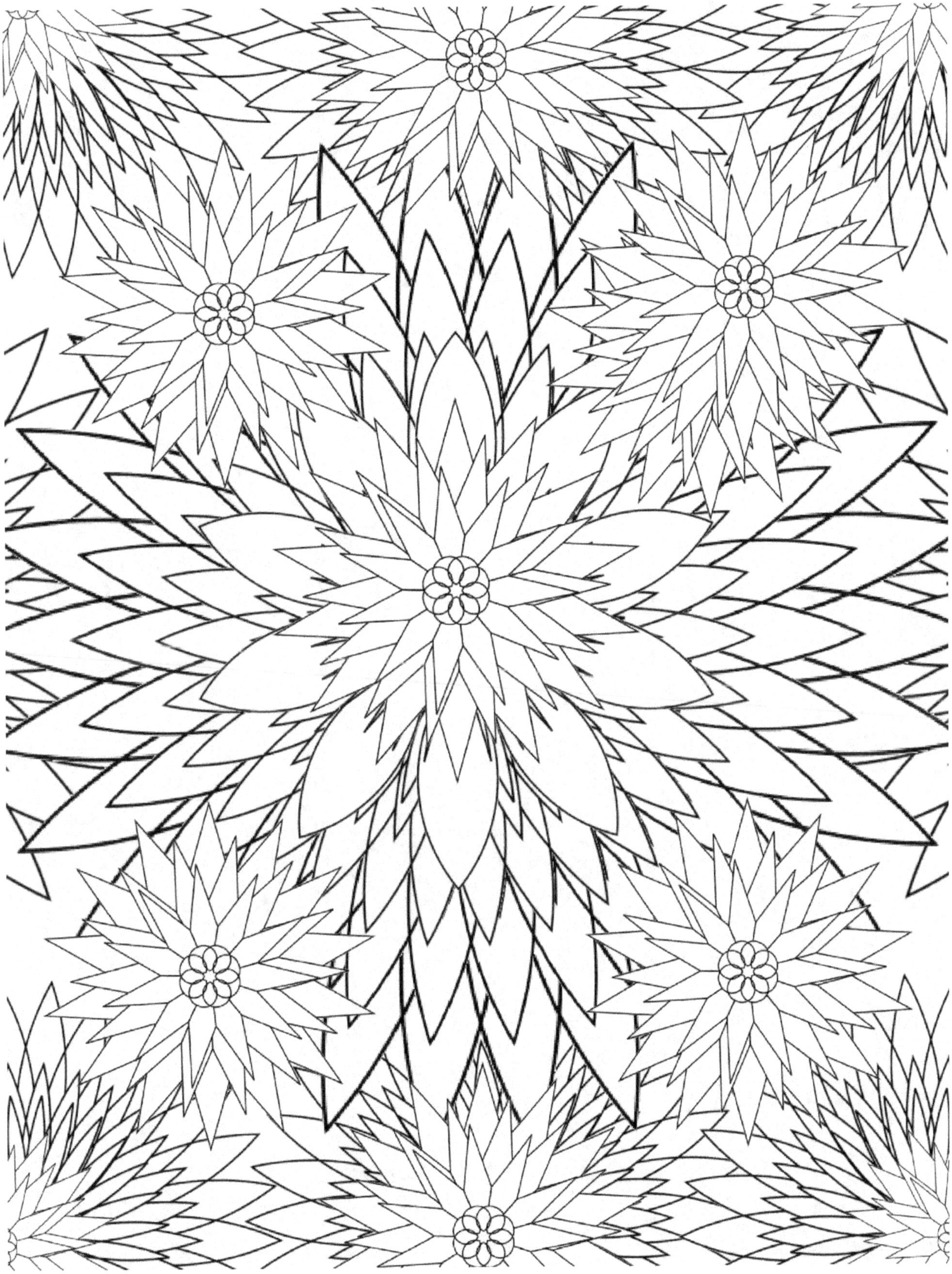

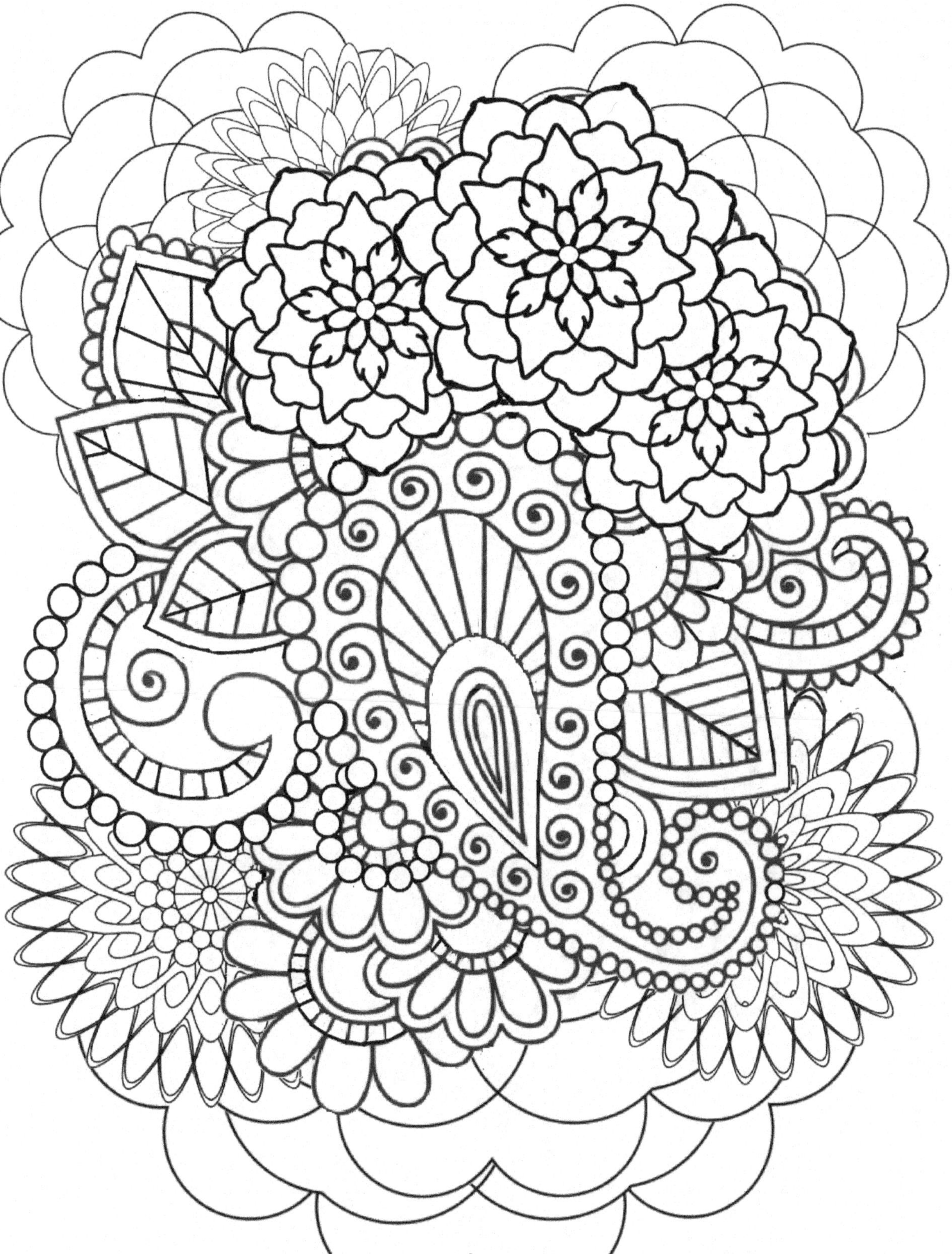

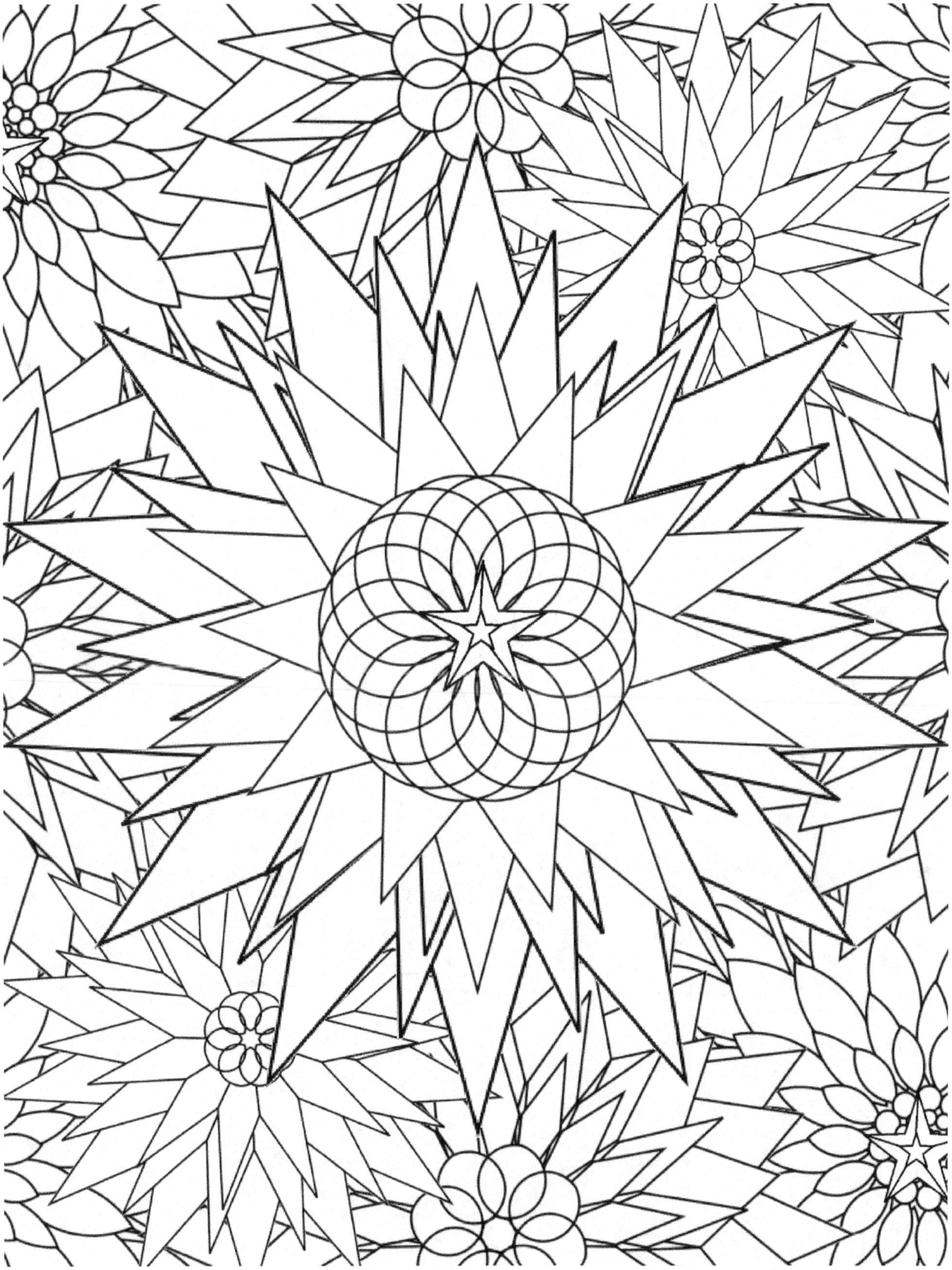

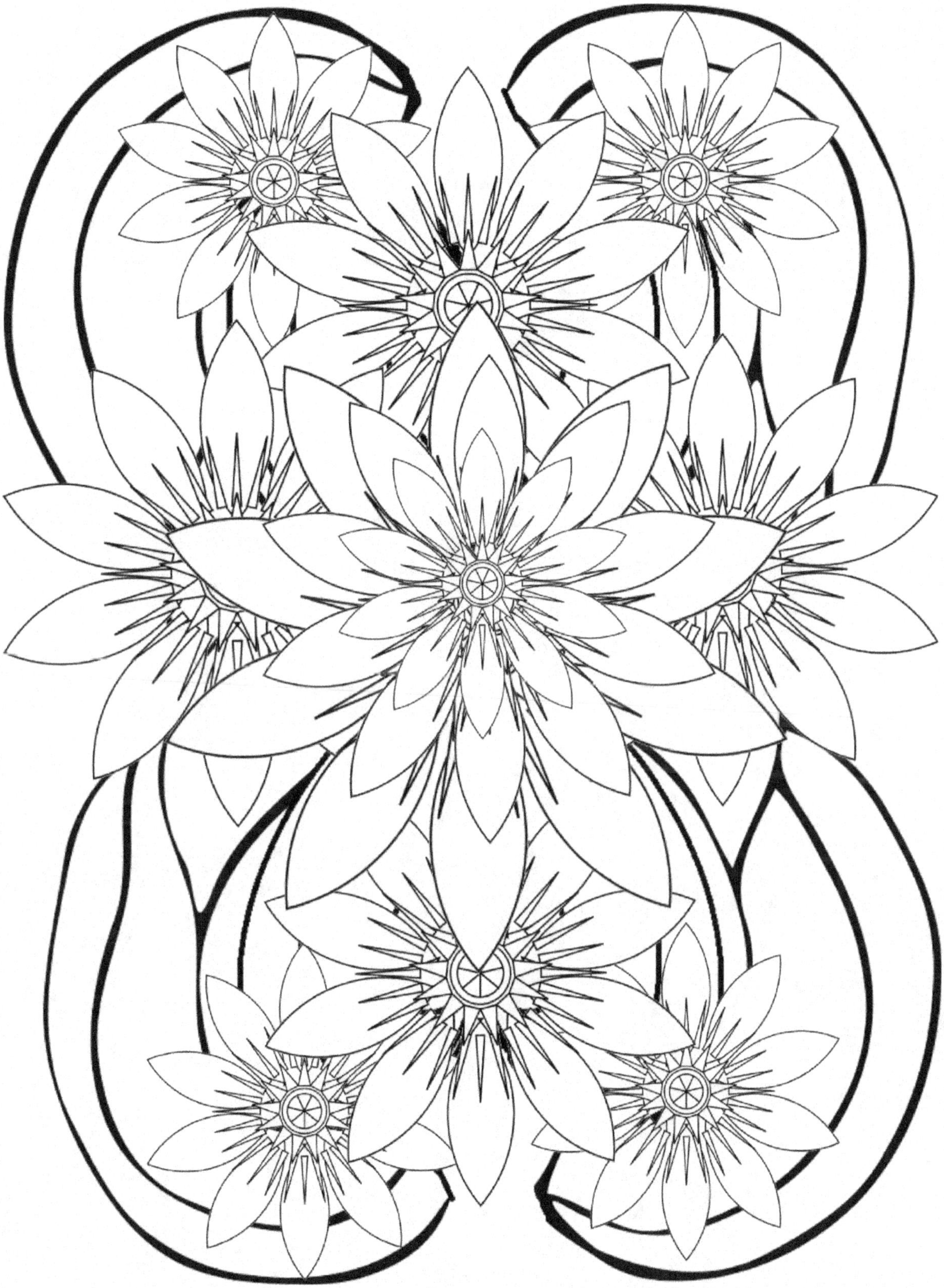

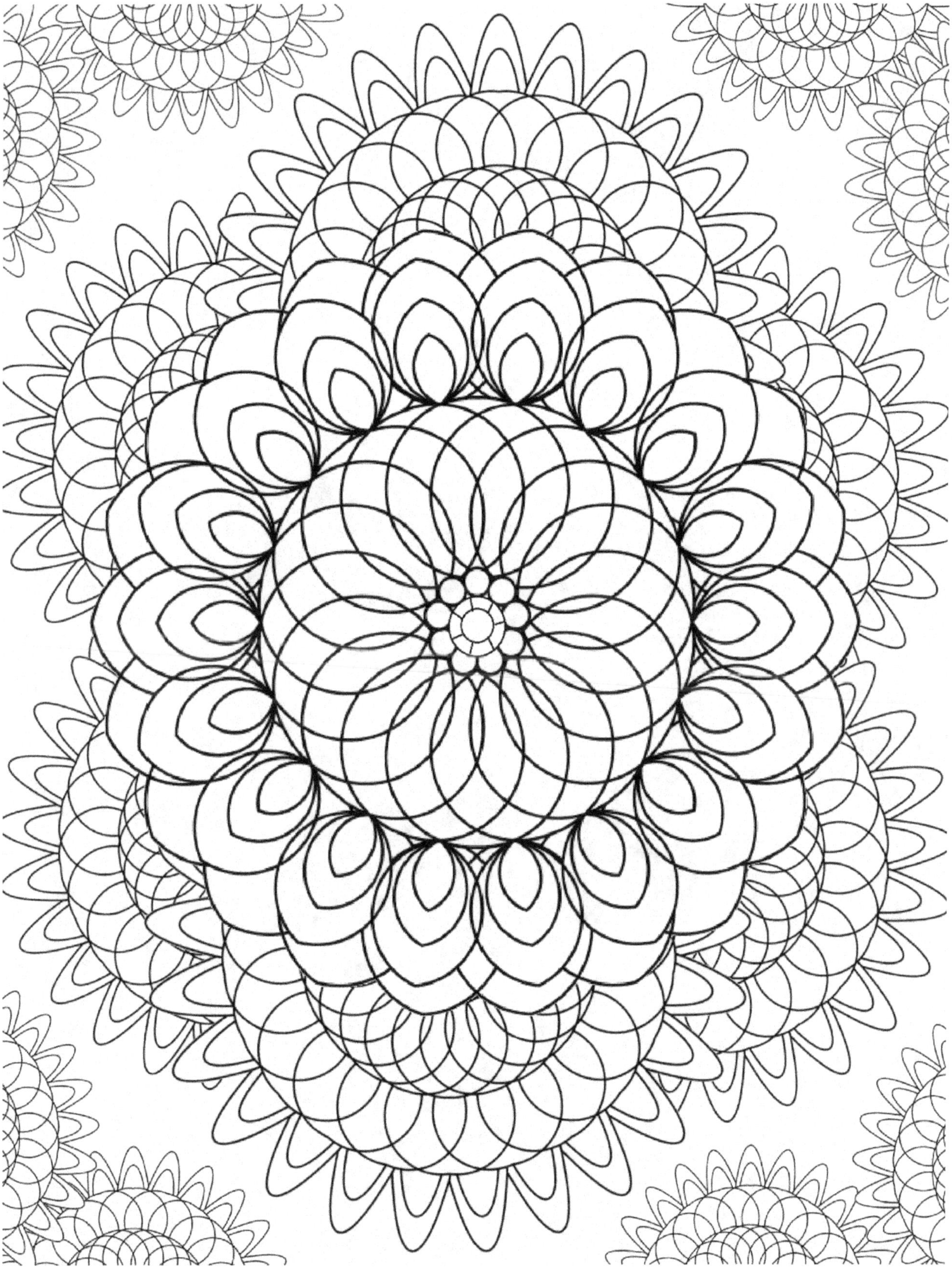

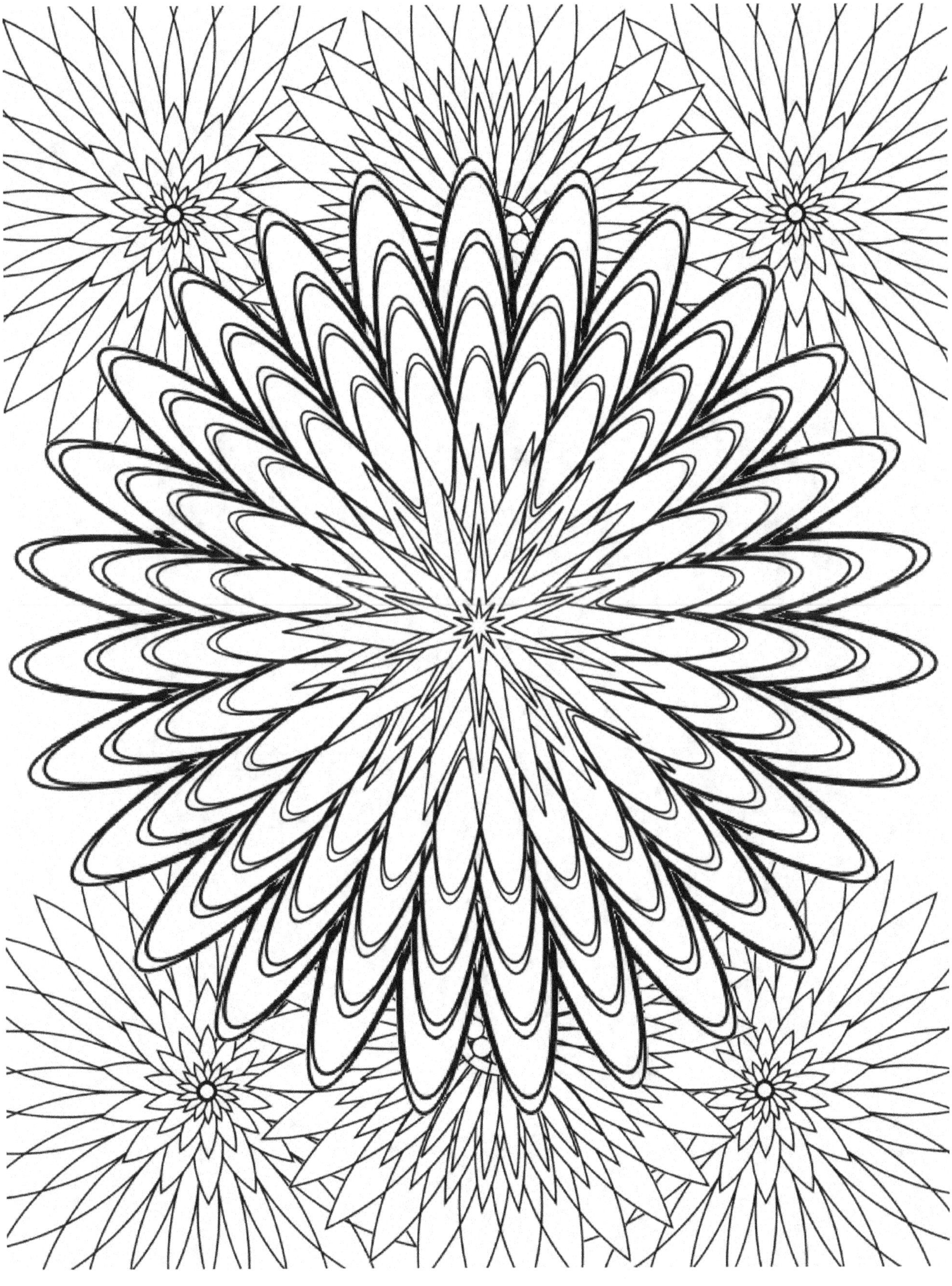

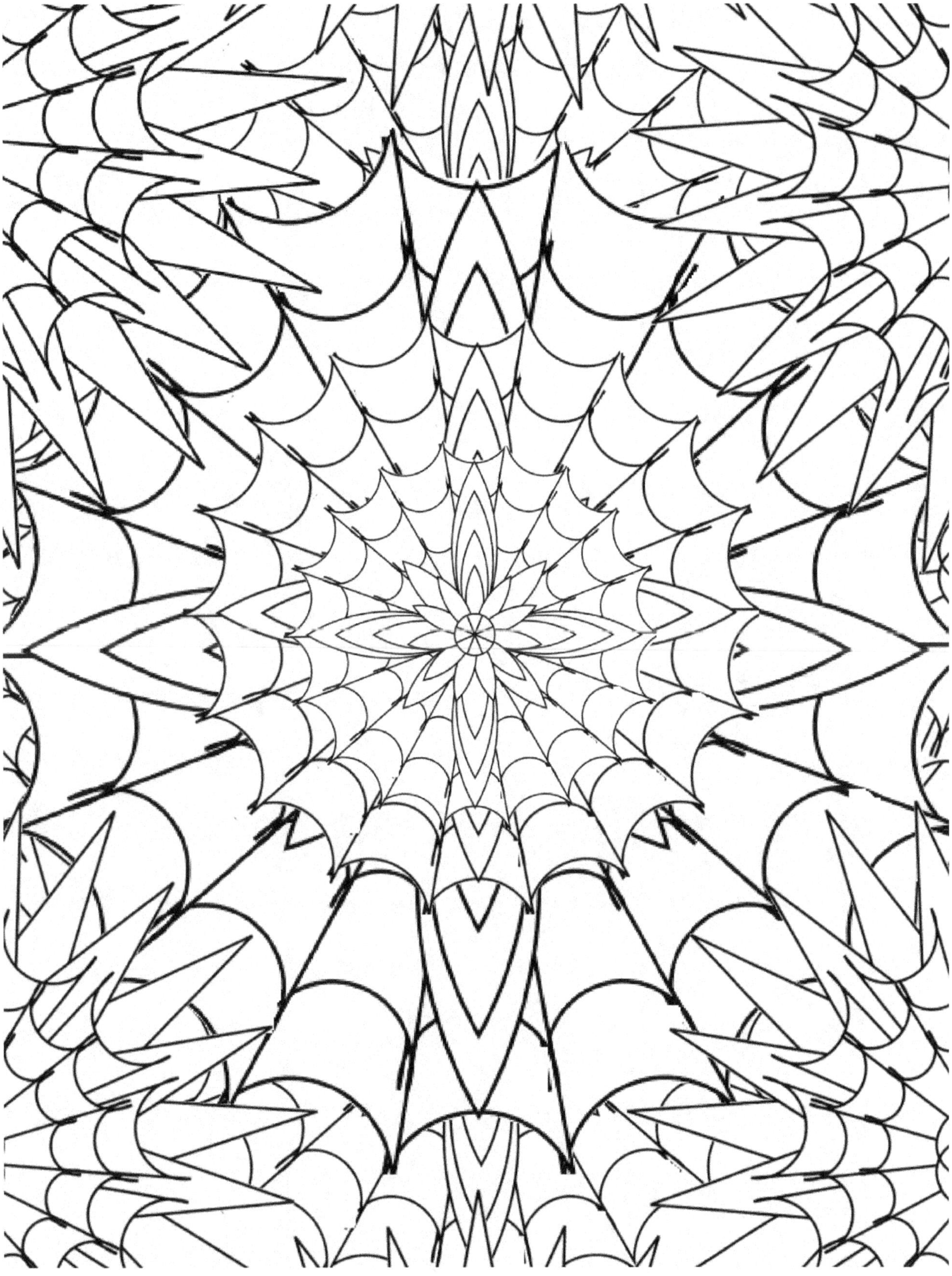

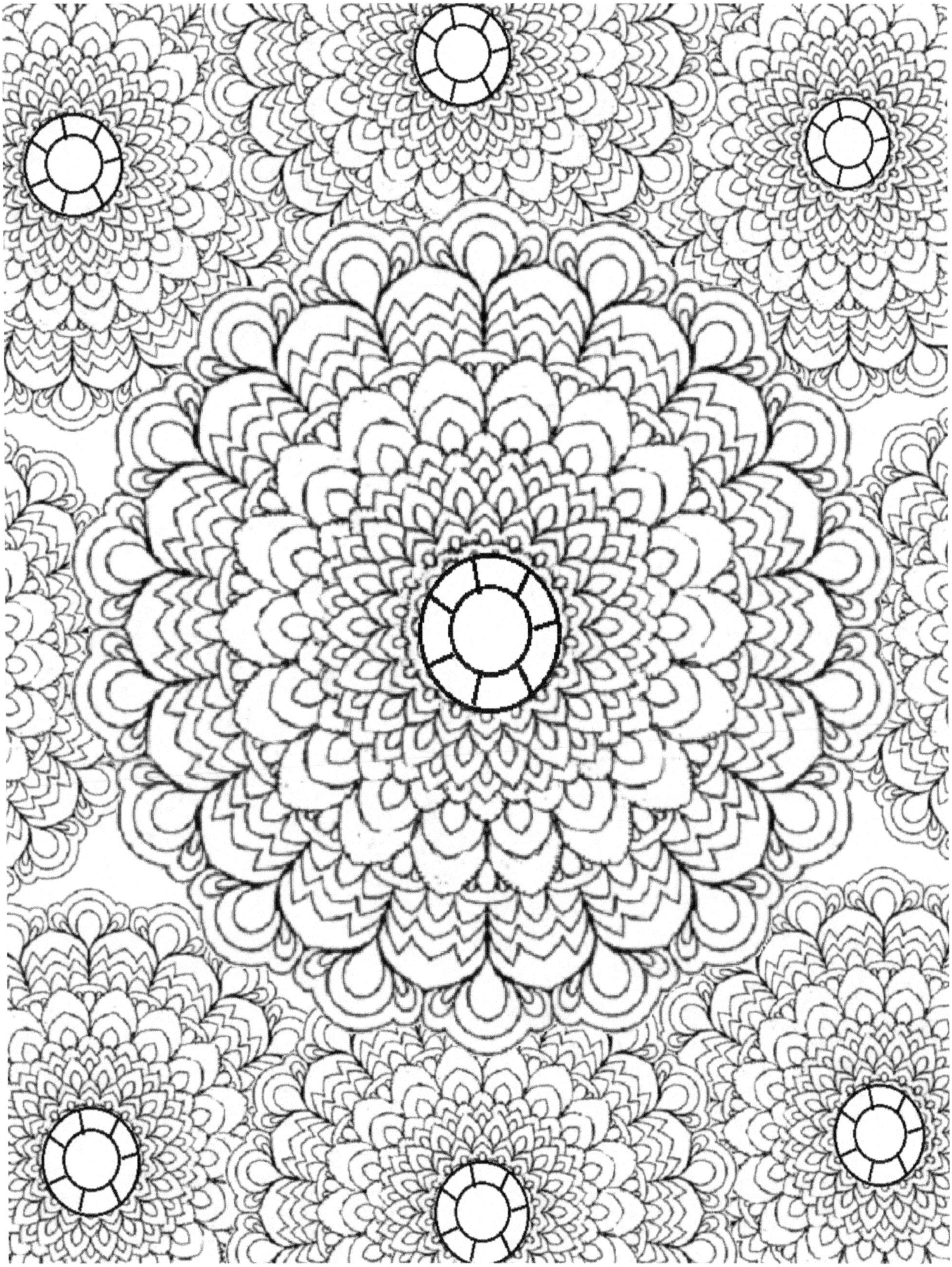

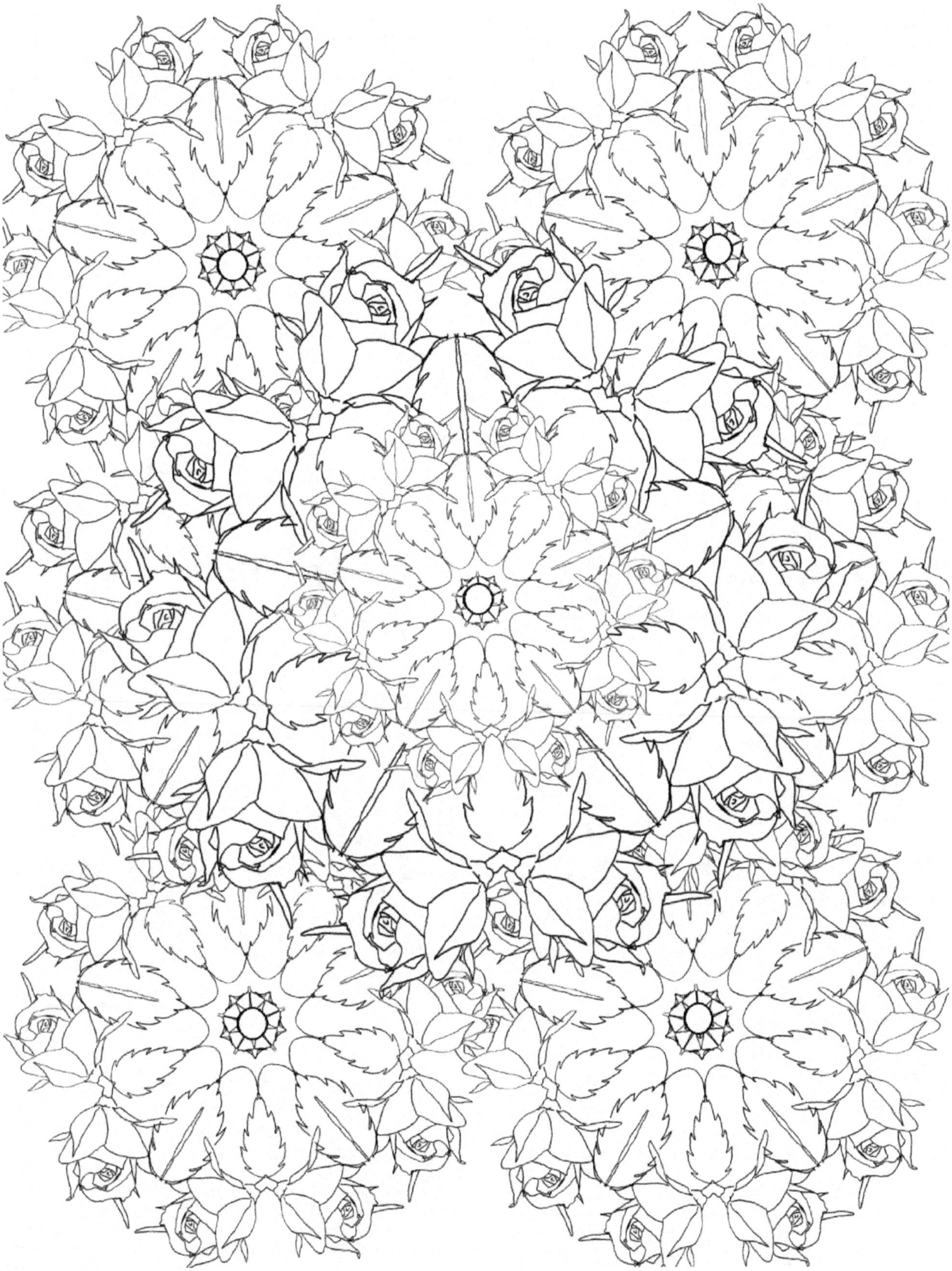

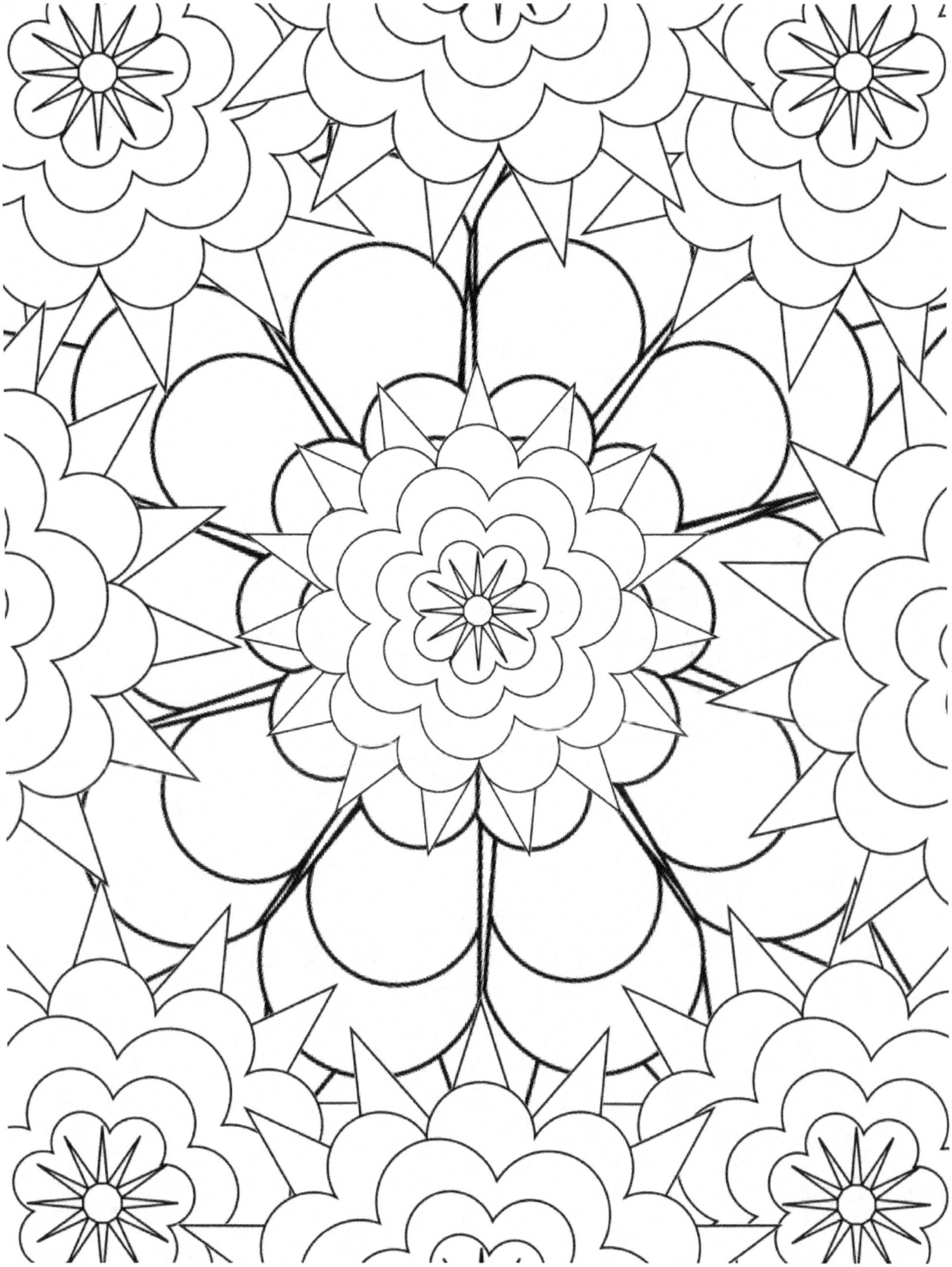

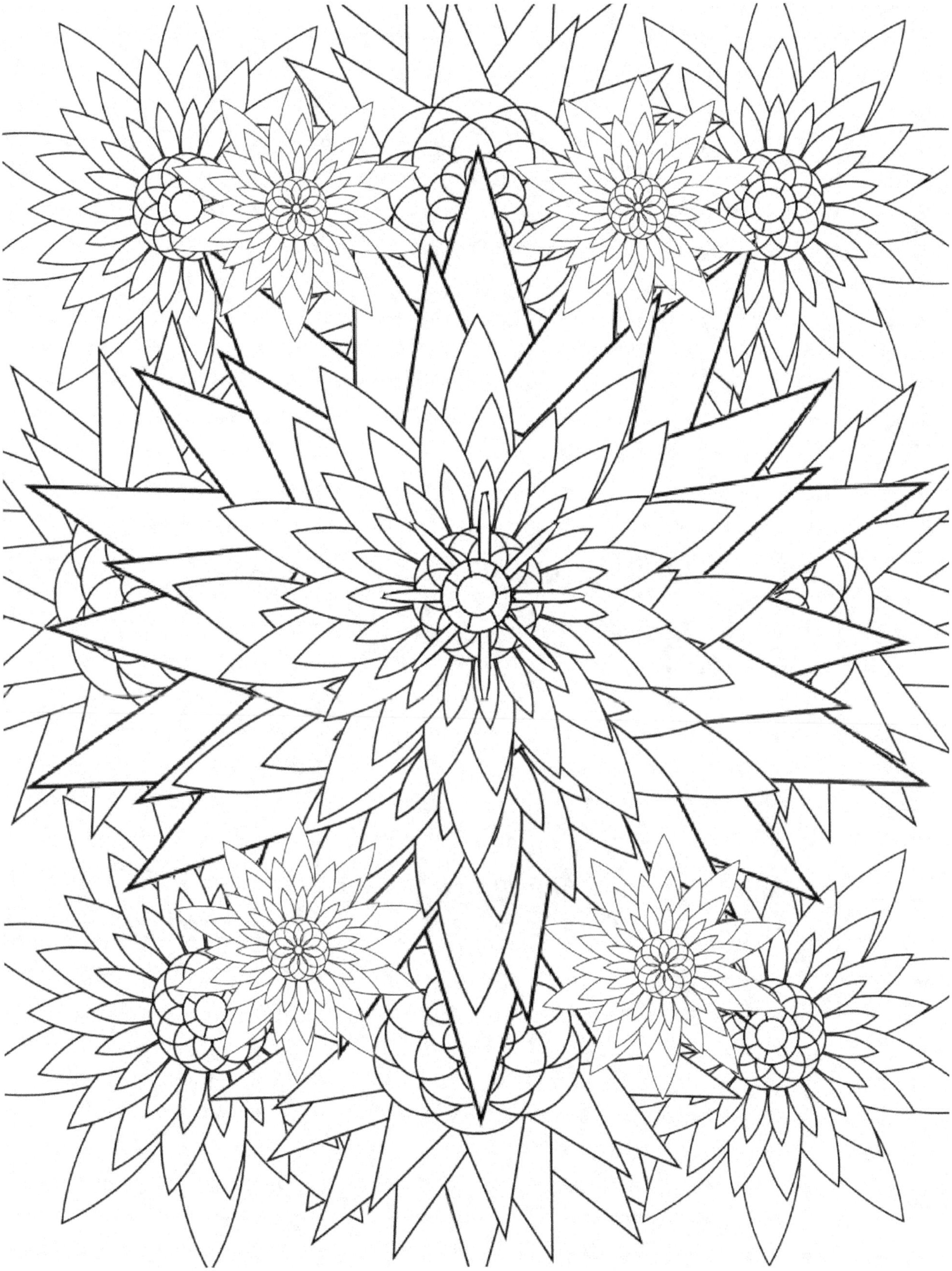

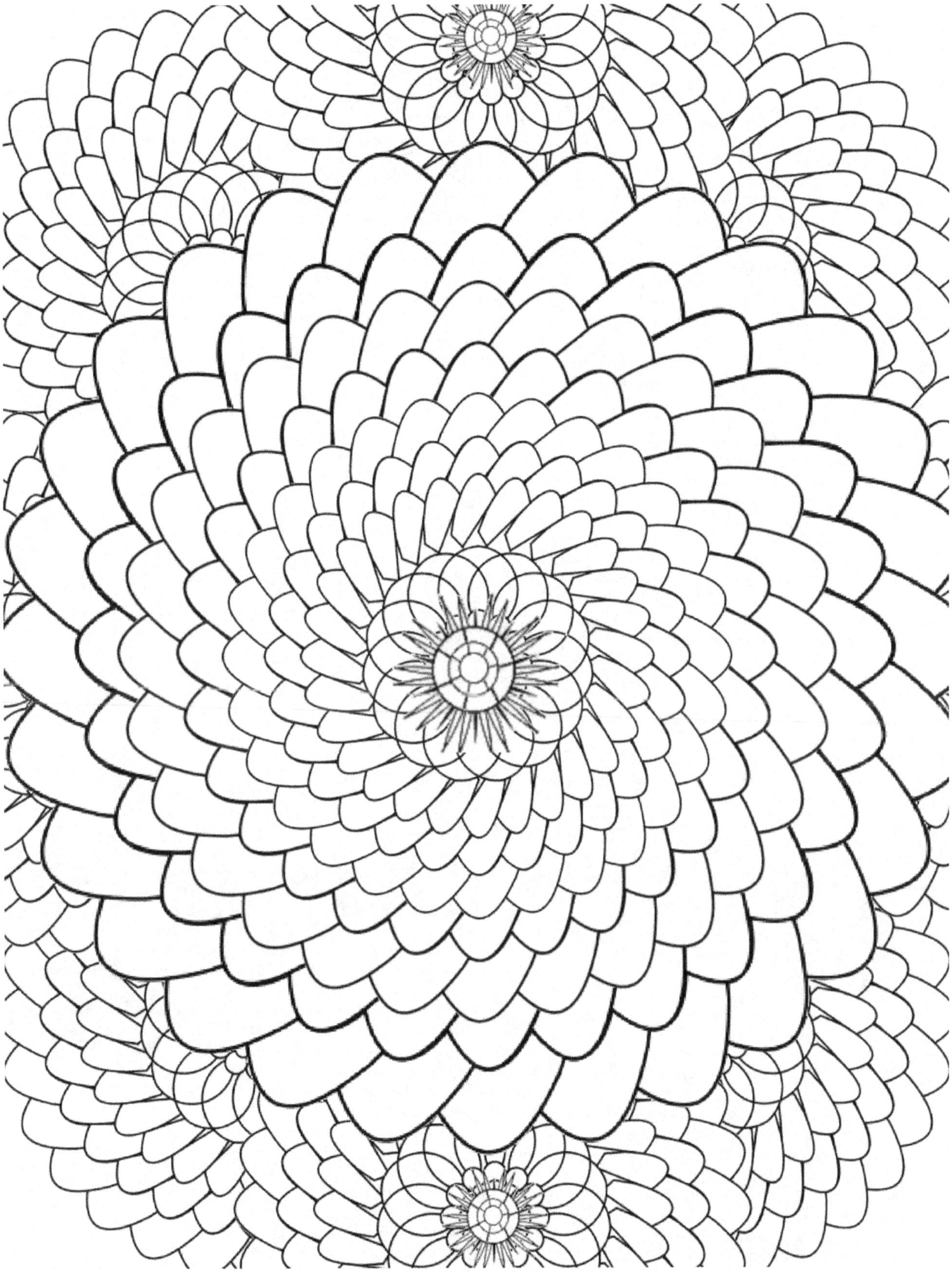

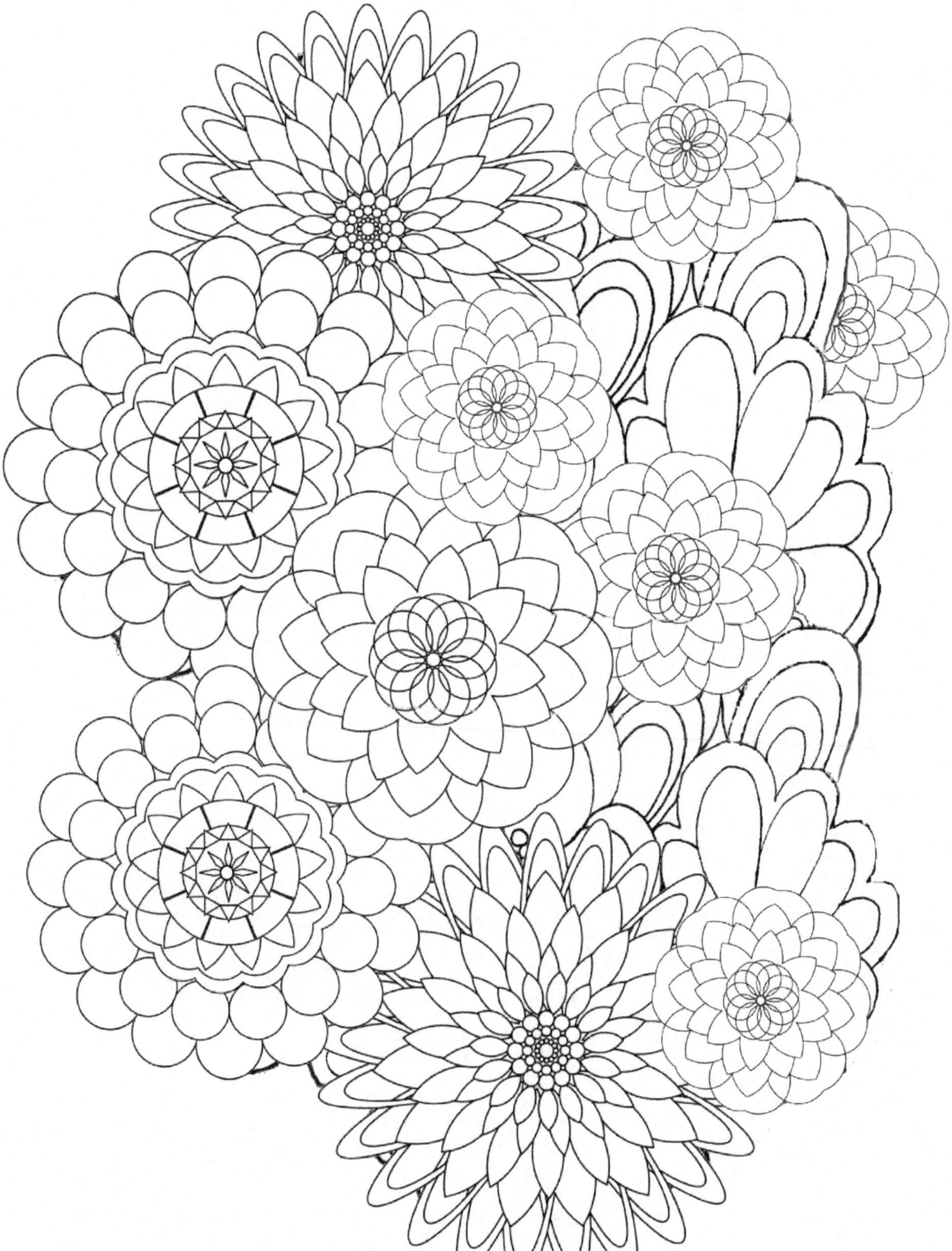

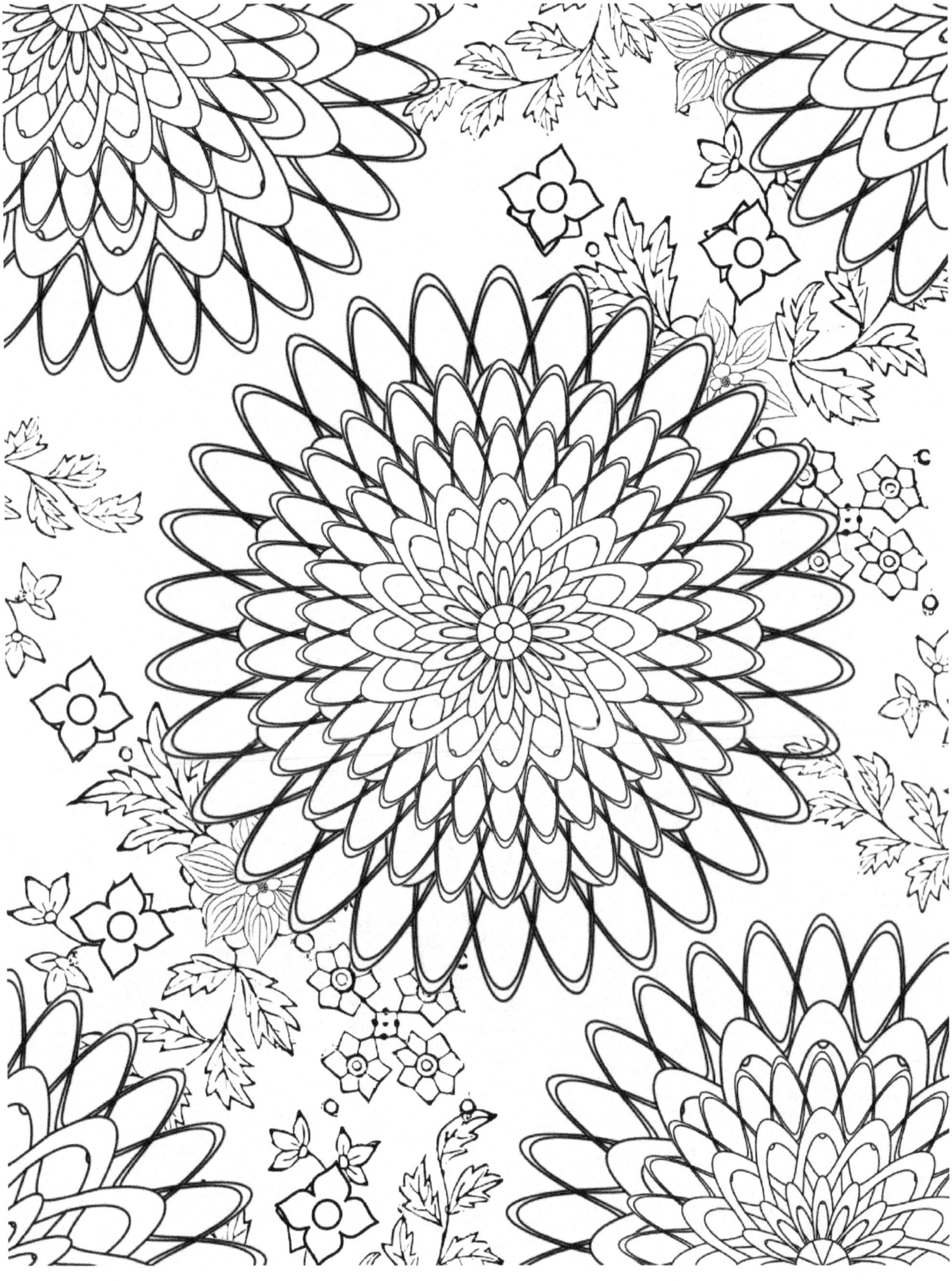

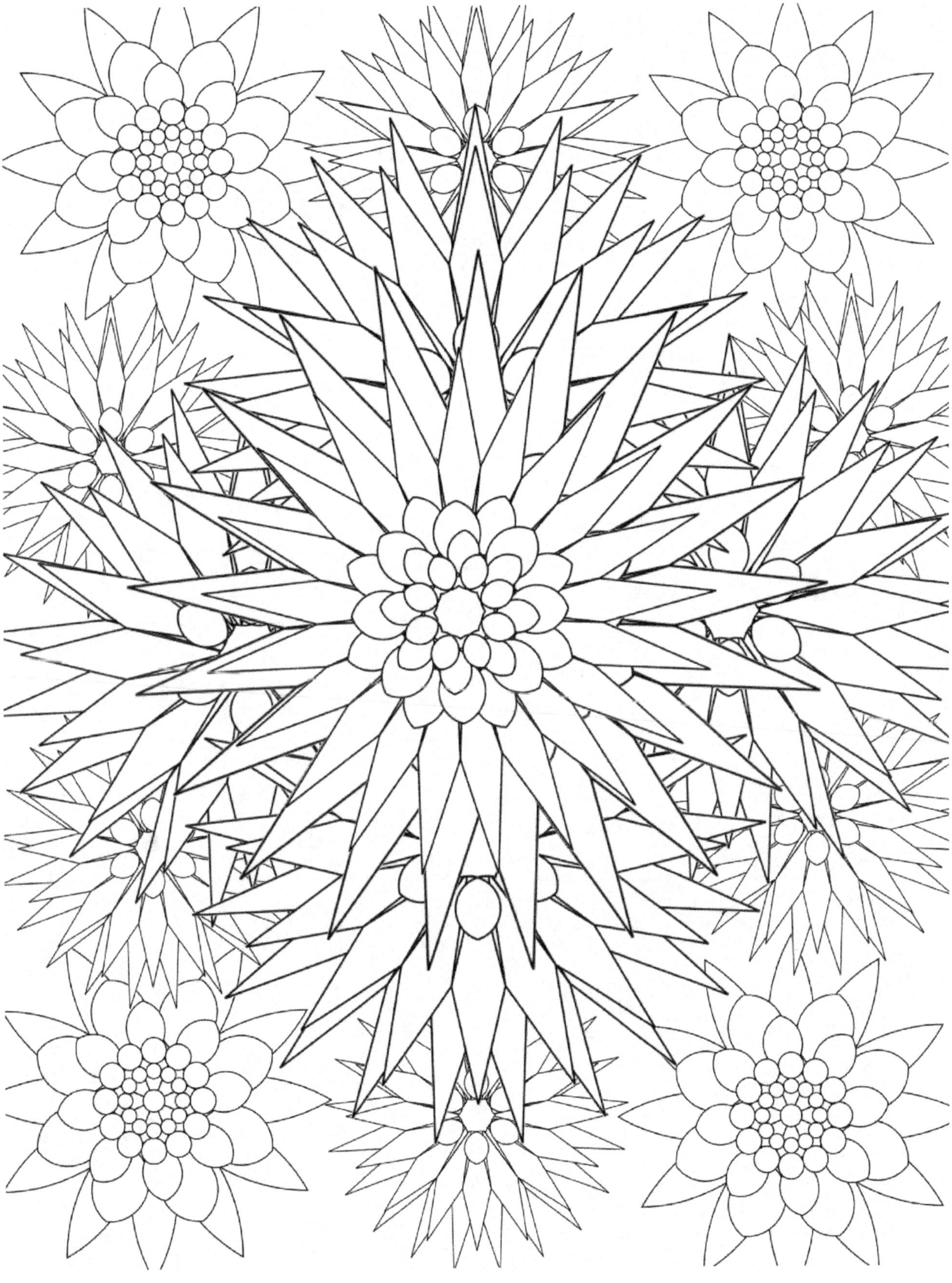

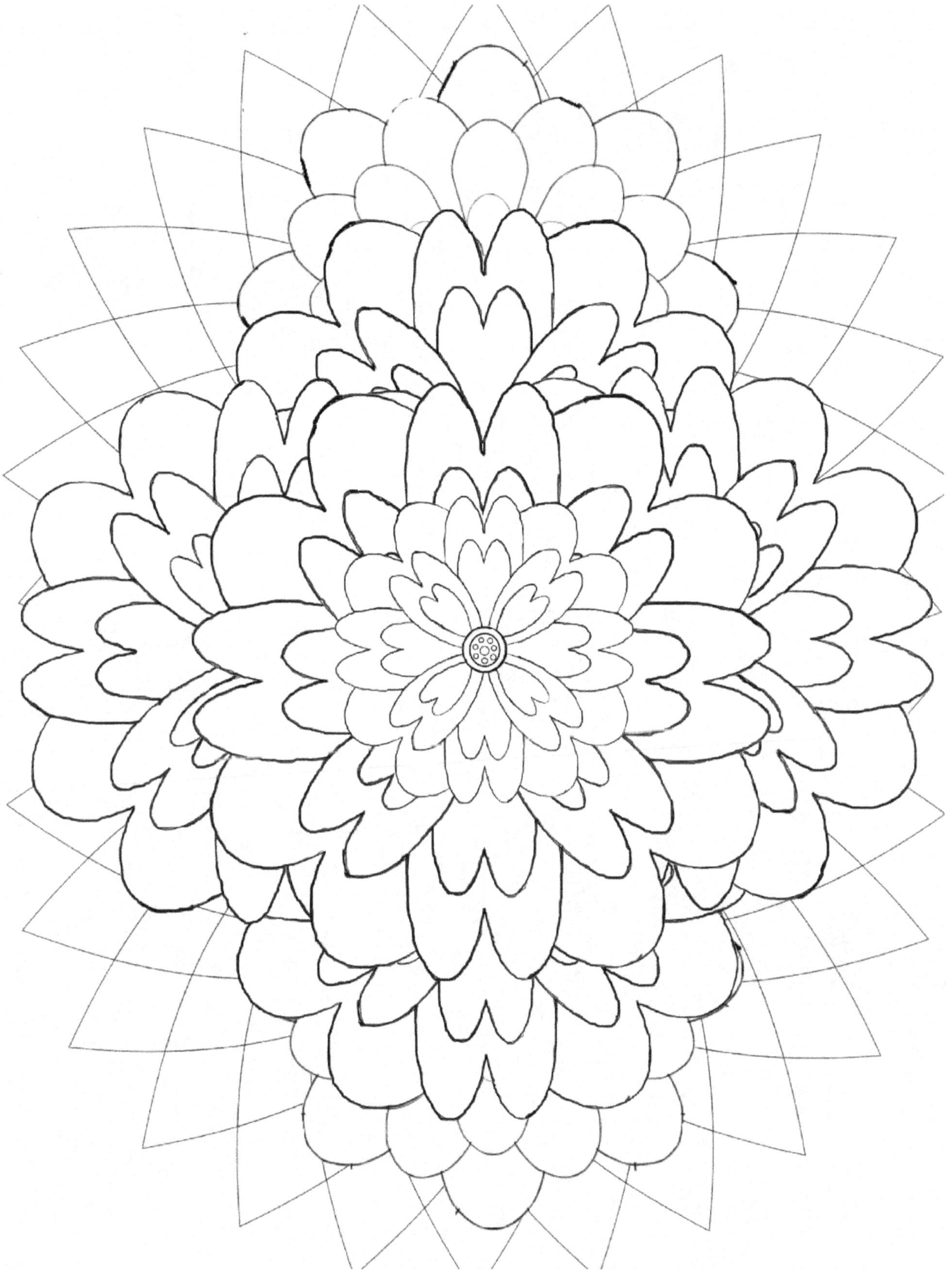

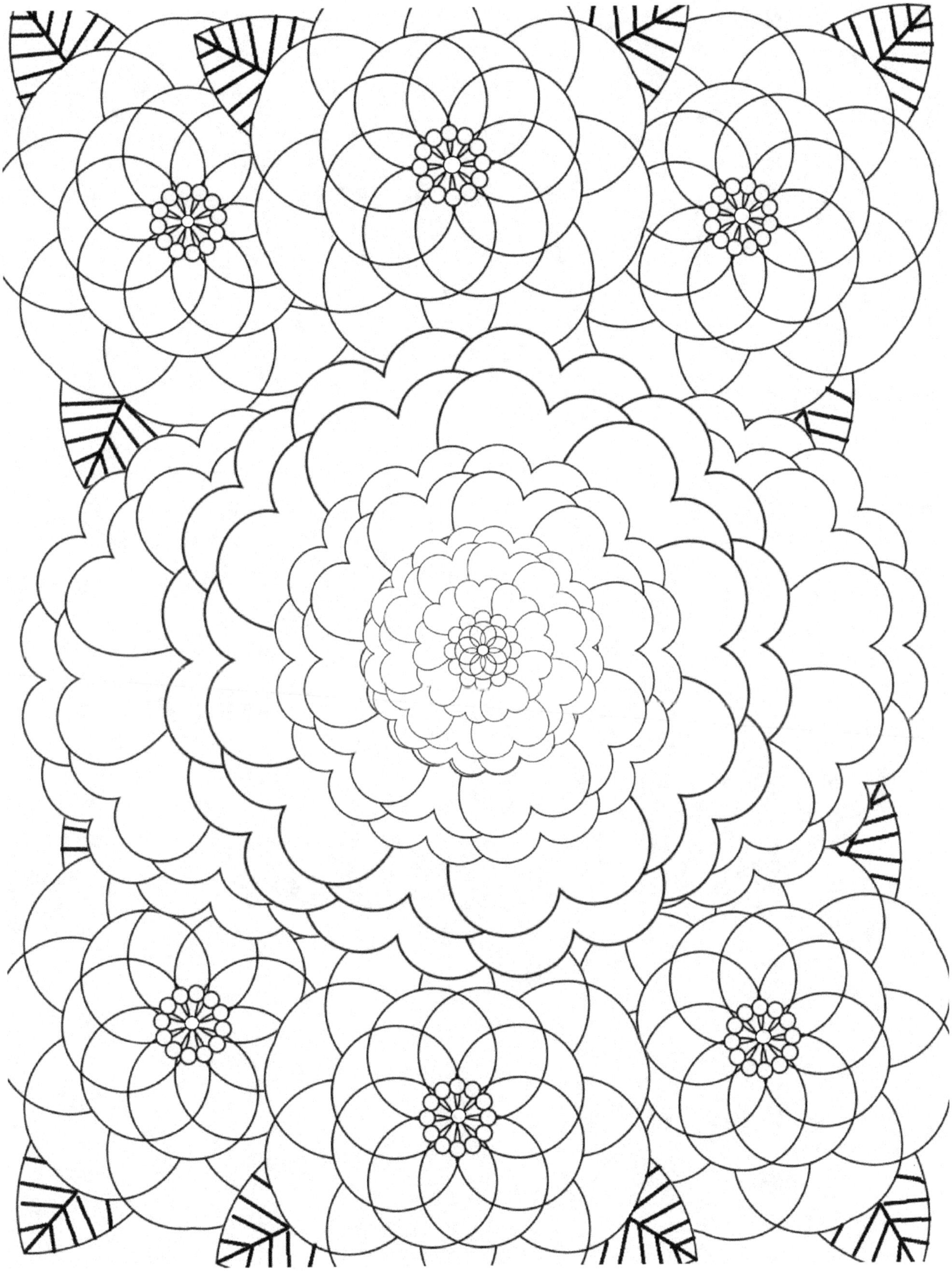

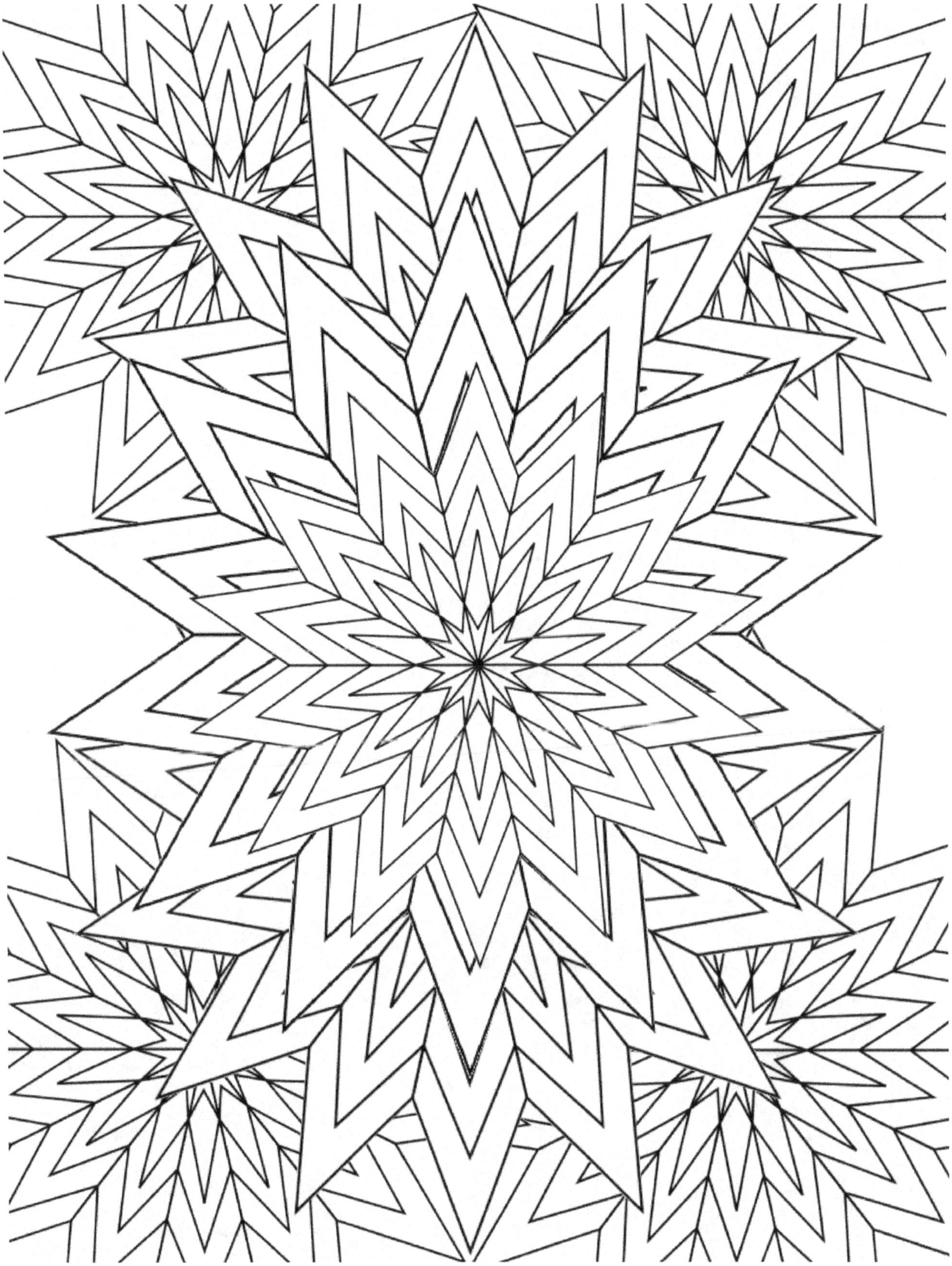

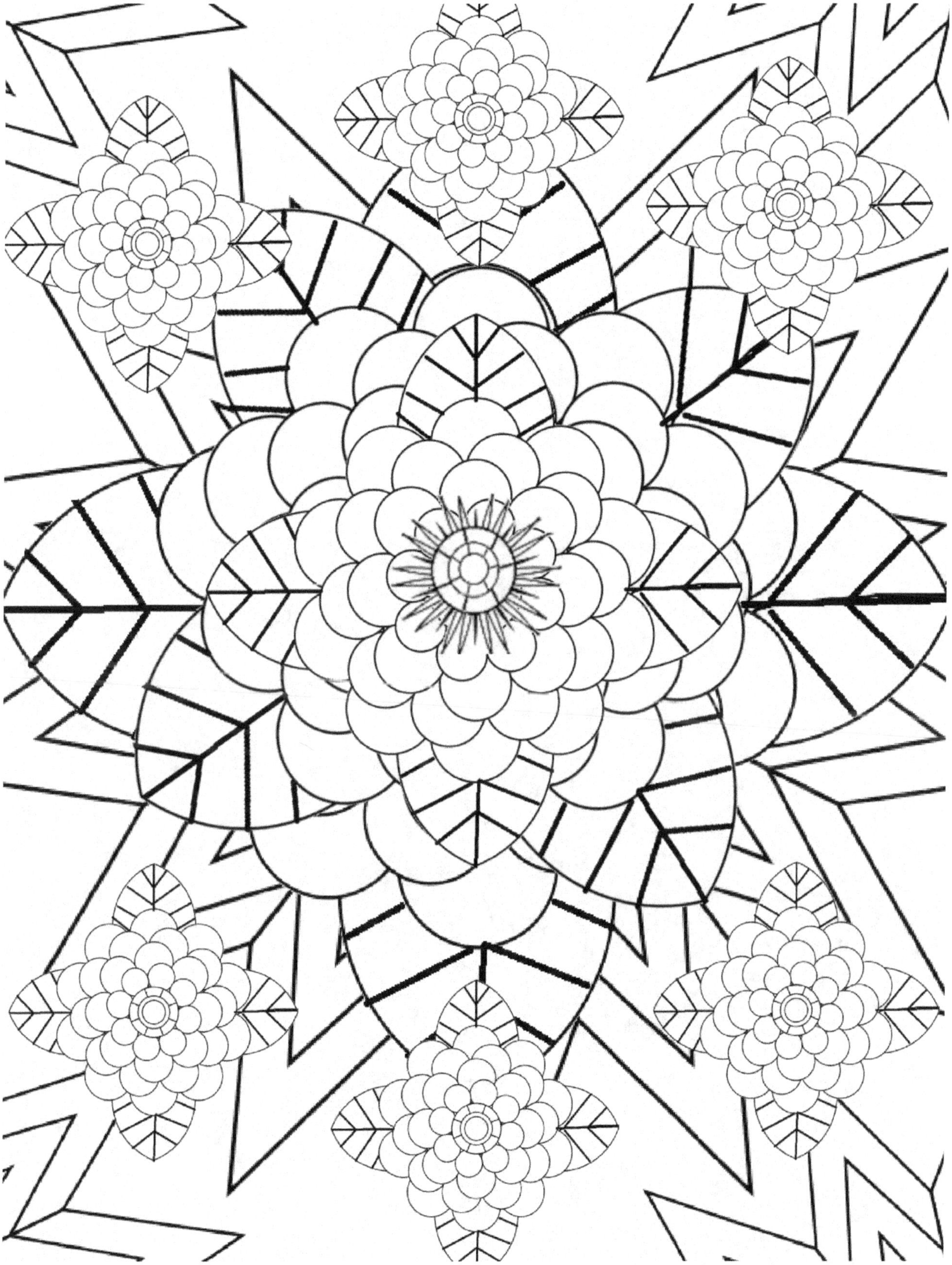

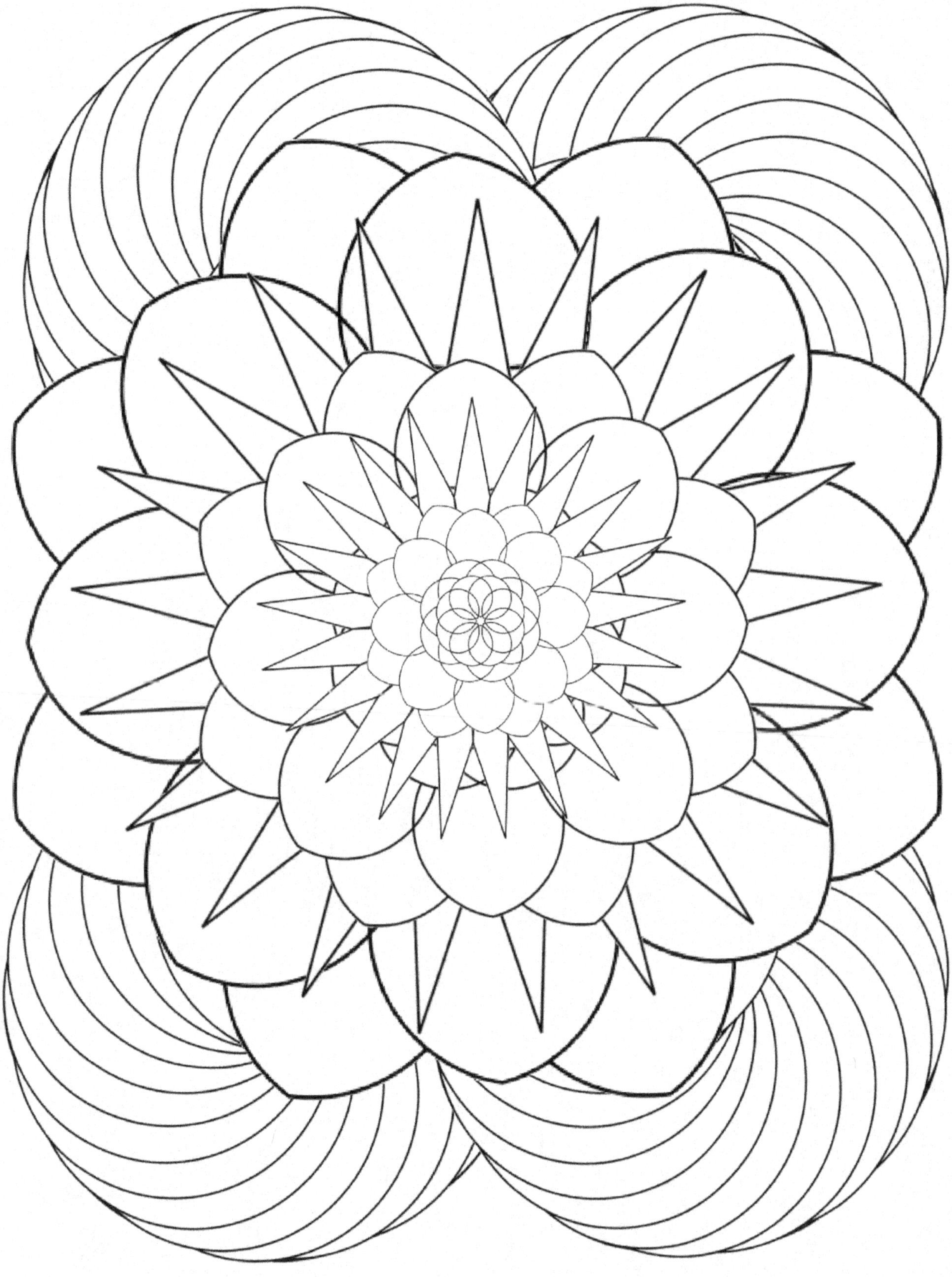

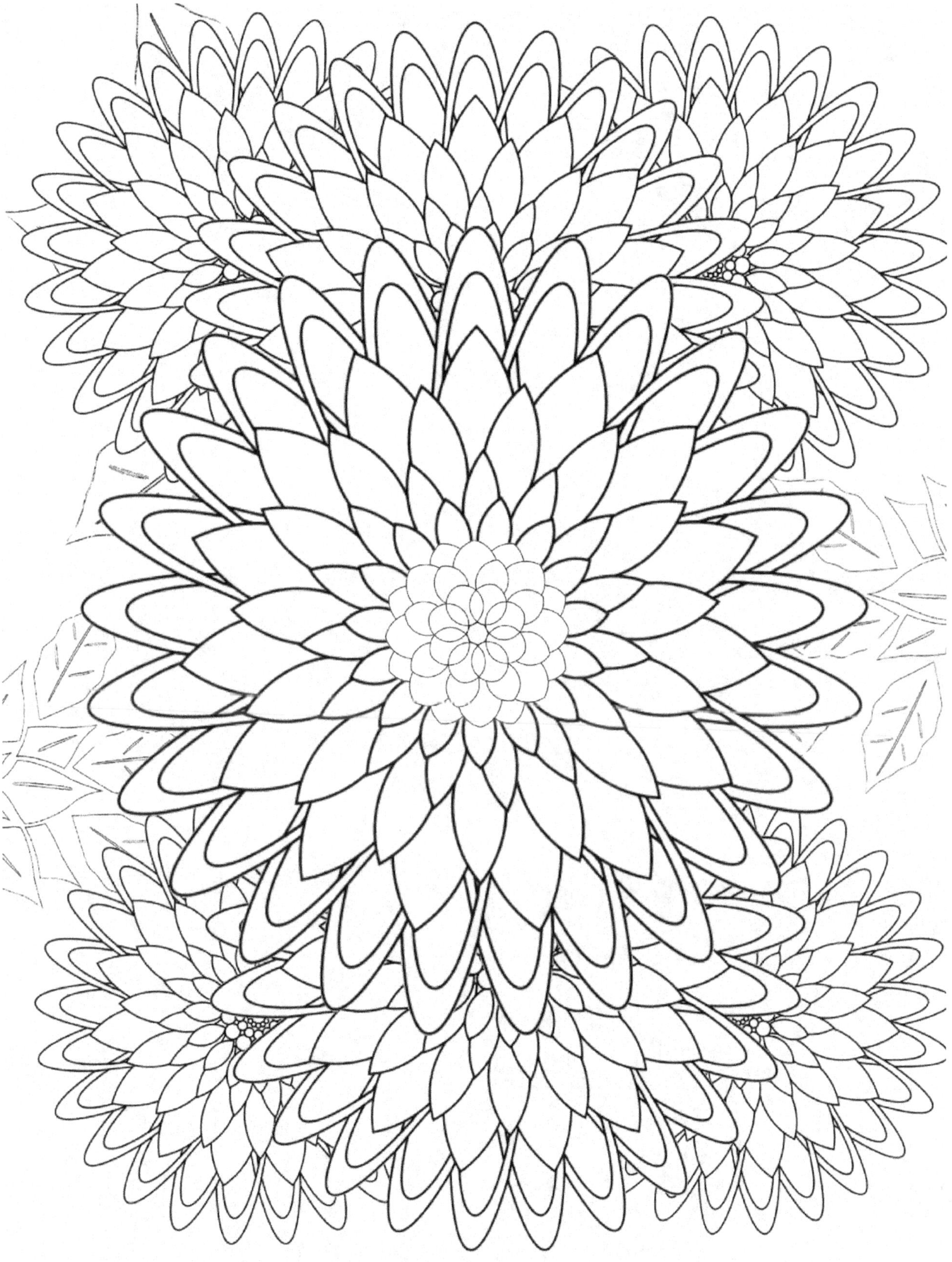

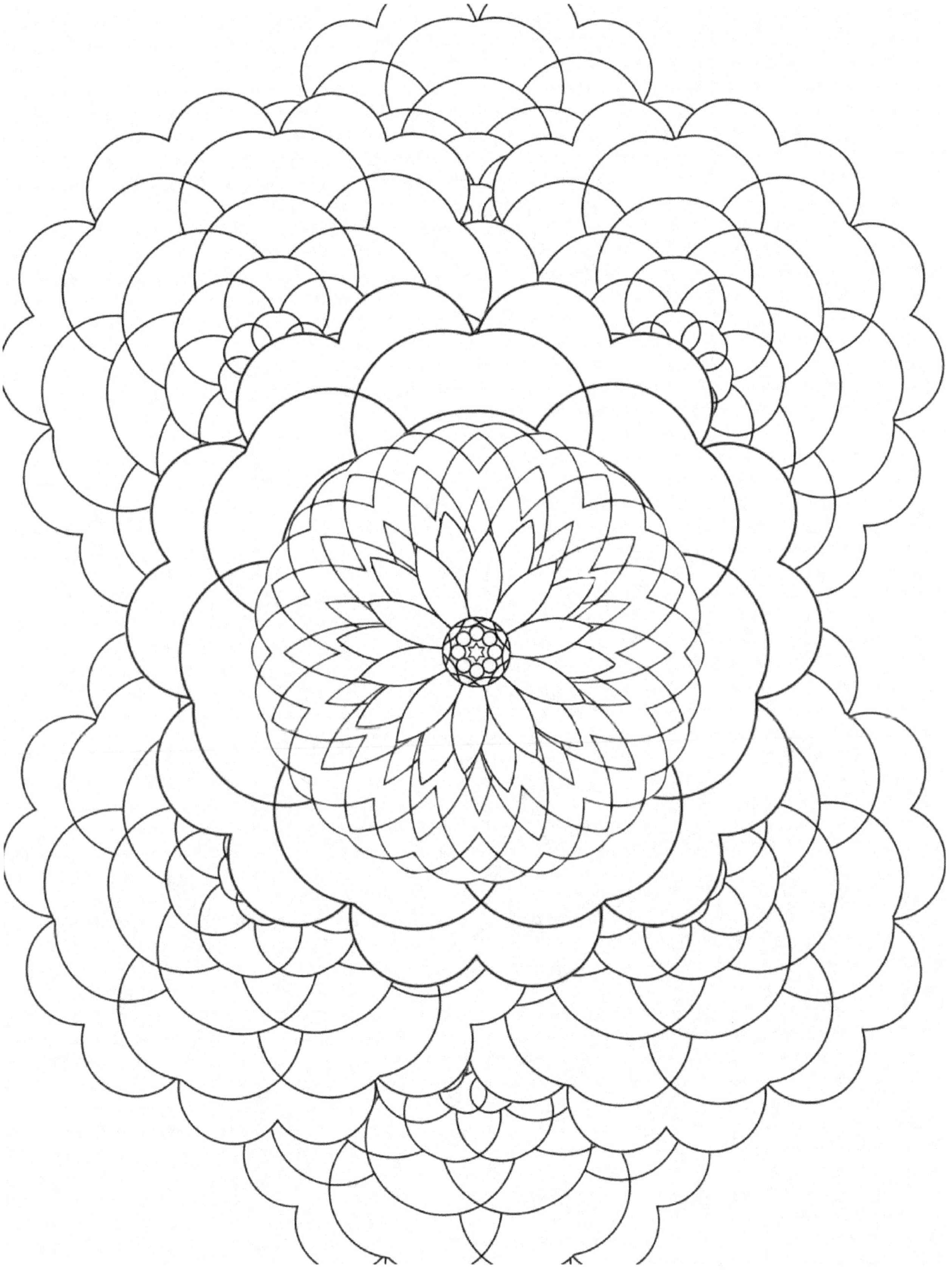

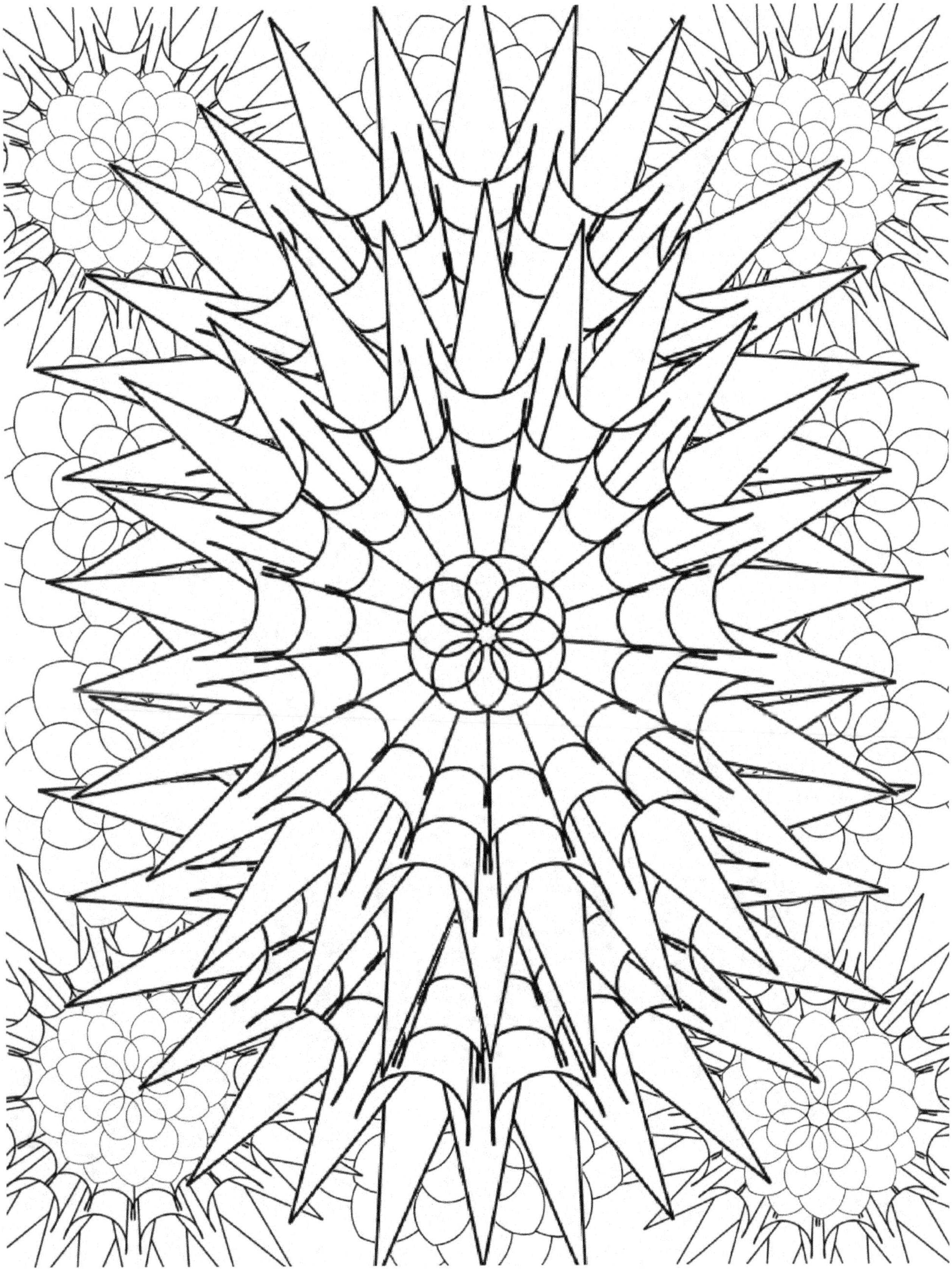

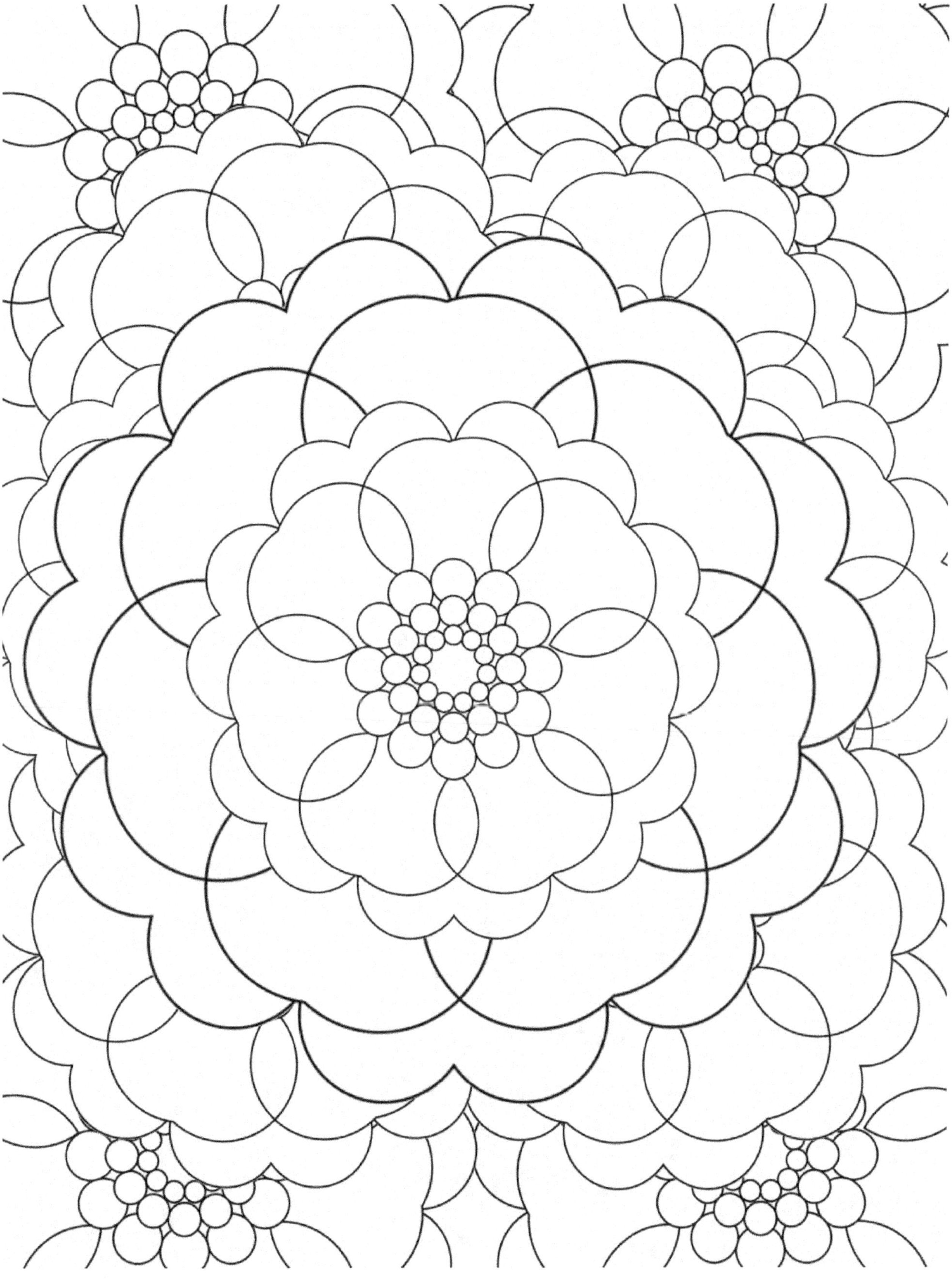

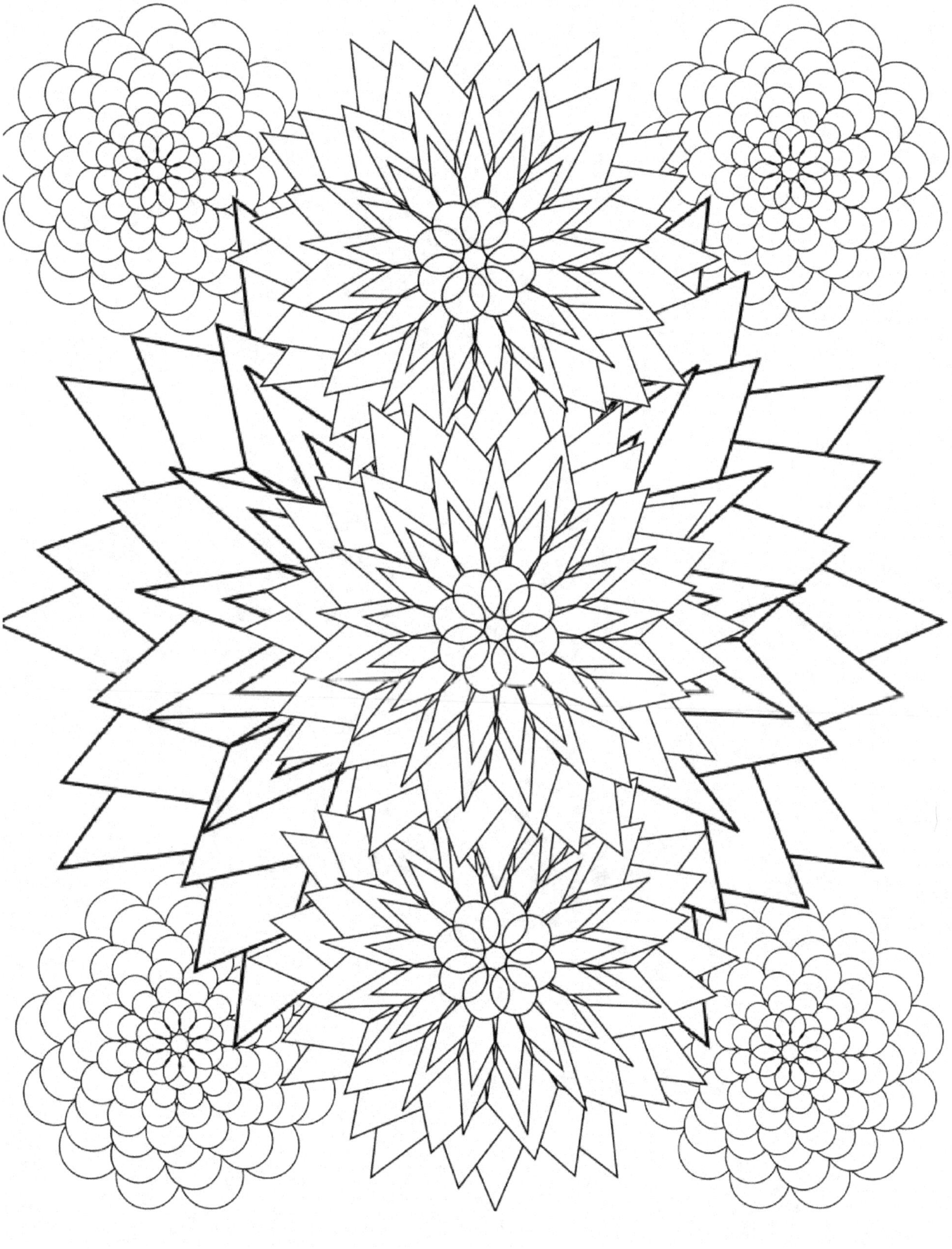

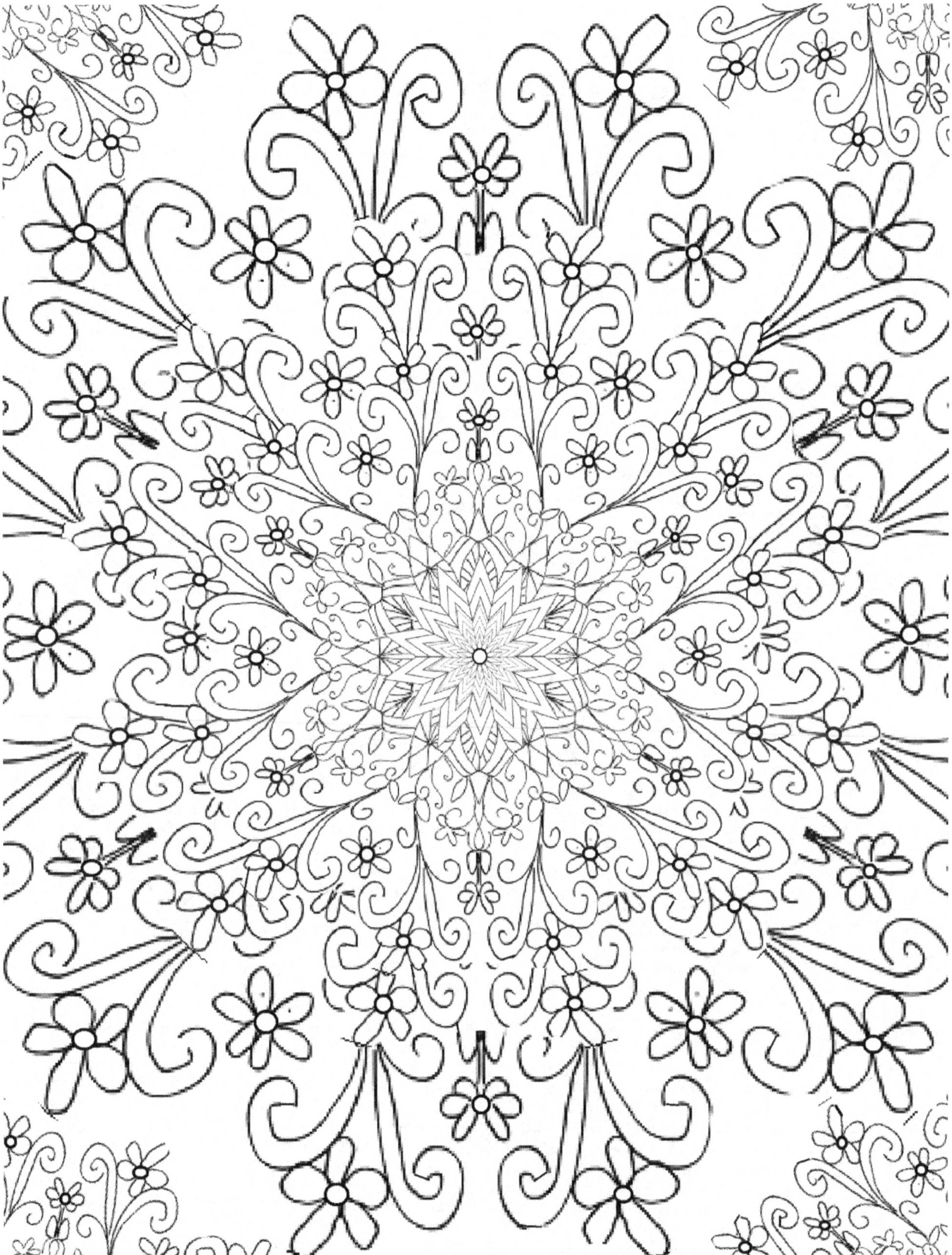

Other Adult Coloring Books By:

Trueheart Designs

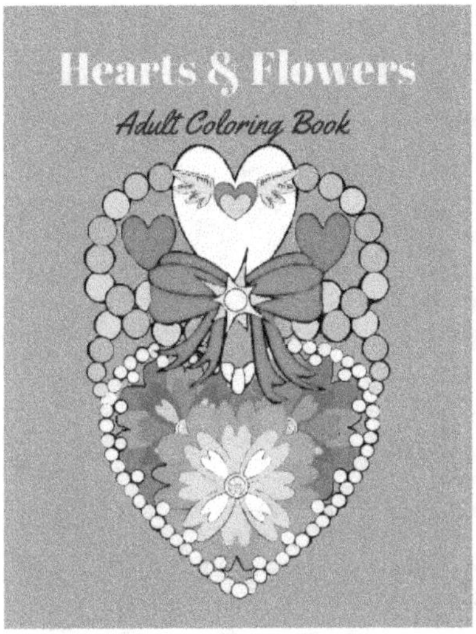

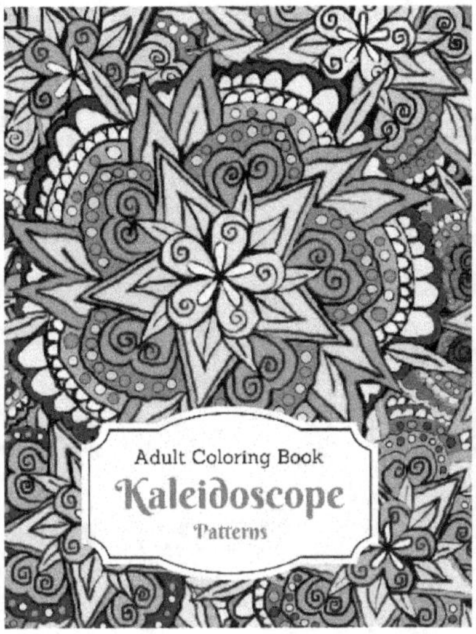

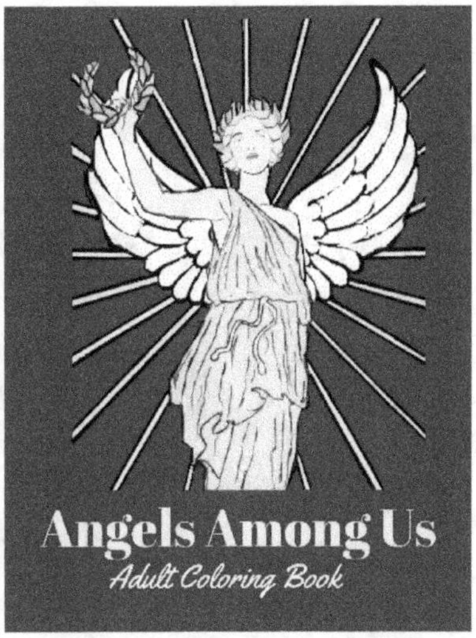

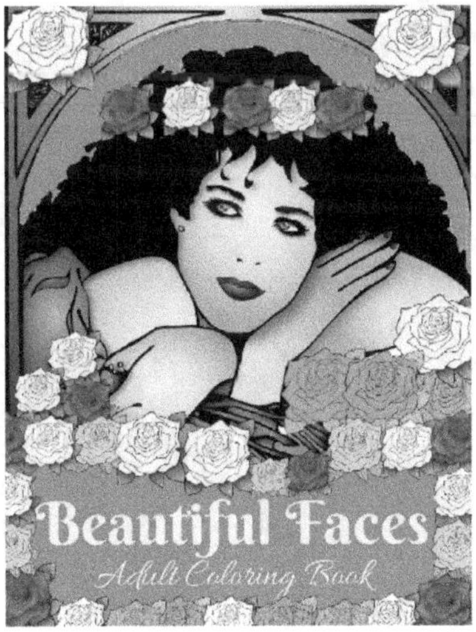

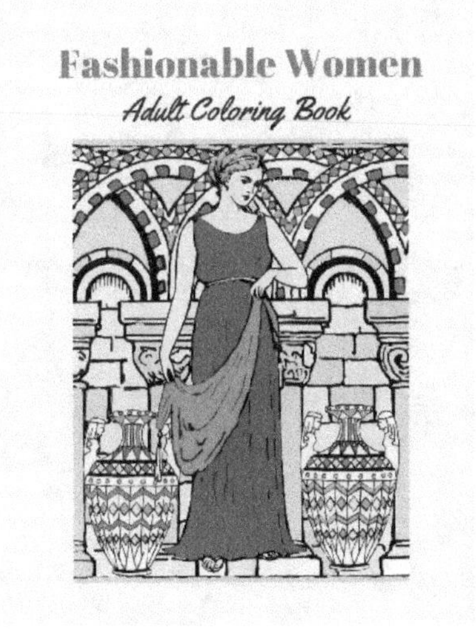

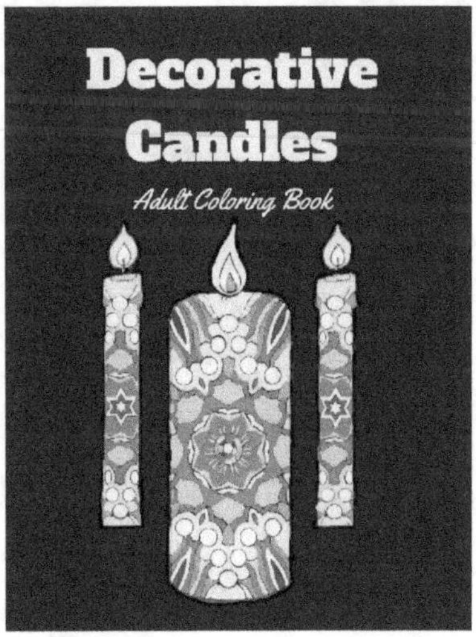

www.ingramcontent.com/pod-product-compliance
Lightning Source LLC
Chambersburg PA
CBHW081225170526
45165CB00009B/2949
* 9 7 8 1 5 4 9 8 8 4 9 6 2 *